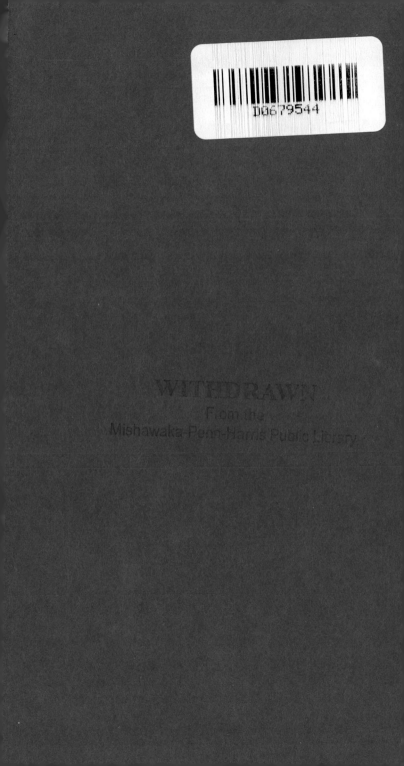

D0679544

A
GENTLEMAN
WALKS DOWN
THE
AISLE

A GENTLEMAN WALKS DOWN *THE* AISLE

A COMPLETE GUIDE TO THE
PERFECT WEDDING DAY

JOHN BRIDGES
and BRYAN CURTIS

THOMAS NELSON
Since 1798

NASHVILLE   DALLAS   MEXICO CITY   RIO DE JANEIRO

Published in Nashville, Tennessee, by Thomas Nelson. Thomas Nelson is a registered trademark of Thomas Nelson, Inc.

Illustrations by Alicia Adkerson, Adkerson Designs

Thomas Nelson, Inc., titles may be purchased in bulk for educational, business, fund-raising, or sales promotional use. For information, please e-mail SpecialMarkets@ThomasNelson.com.

Library of Congress Cataloging-in-Publication Data

Bridges, John, 1950–
  A gentleman walks down the aisle : a complete guide to the perfect wedding day / John Bridges and Bryan Curtis.
      p. cm.
  Includes bibliographical references and index.
  ISBN 978-1-4016-0063-1 (alk. paper)
  1. Etiquette for men. 2. Bridegrooms. 3. Wedding attendants. 4. Weddings.
5. Wedding etiquette. I. Curtis, Bryan, 1960– II. Title. III. Title: Complete guide to the perfect wedding day.
  BJ1855.B75 2011
  395.2'2081—dc22   2010051517

Printed in the United States of America

11 12 13 14 15 WOR 6 5 4 3 2 1

For Krista and Todd, who helped start this book when they started down the aisle

—J. B.

For Keith Merrill and Angie Jones. A gentleman couldn't ask for better friends.

—B. C.

CONTENTS

INTRODUCTION

A marriage is generally deemed to be about two people—two people who have decided to spend the rest of their lives together, sharing the joys, the pleasures, and the challenges of the coming years.

Likewise, the wedding that begins that lifetime of shared joys, pleasures, and challenges is ostensibly about those same two people. But experience and honest observation have taught us that, in most cases, that is not accurate. The groom may have been the one who actually got the romantic ball rolling by asking an attractive acquaintance out for a quiet dinner, followed by a movie and perhaps a glass of wine. He may have been the one who waited for the perfect moment to take the quivering hand in his and pop the question, having already gone on the hunt for the perfect diamond, one that would match the winsome glitter in her eye. He and his intended may have sat down and talked forthrightly about the wedding they want—whether it will take place in a house of worship, in the garden of a lovely home, or in front of a judge at city hall. He may assume that this wedding will be a joint effort, merely a first glimpse of their life together in the years to come.

The groom will probably want to think again. As the happy day grows nearer, any mention of "Jason and Mary Sue's wedding" will have been absorbed into "Mary Sue's wedding." Somehow, the questions about his choice of dinner jacket, and all the preliminary talk about "the simple, perfect ceremony—the moment of a lifetime, just for the two of us and the people we really cherish" will have dissolved into a haze of white tulle, clever party invitations, suggested menus from the caterer, and endless hand-wringing over just how many people really can be seated at the ceremony.

More than once, the groom will have every good reason to feel like the forgotten man of the hour—a cog in the great wheel of marital merrymaking, just a necessary means to an end, a guy whose only function is to show up and say, "Well, yes, I think I do."

He and the other gentlemen involved in the world of a wedding need not feel so benignly neglected. They need not feel ignored or unnecessary. They do, after all, have roles in the ritual—whether it is an all-out extravaganza or the "simple, perfect ceremony" it started out to be. And their roles are every bit as important as the arranging of the flowers or the selection of the type font for the wedding invitation.

Because the groom and his fellow gentlemen may find themselves left to their own devices as the wedding day approaches, this book is here to help. For the groom himself, the fathers of the bride and groom, the best man, the groom's other attendants, and even the gentleman who participates in the celebration as a guest, this book explains what to do, where to stand, what to wear, and what to say.

Very likely, even if it is intended to be totally untraditional, the wedding day will seem like a full-scale production directed by someone other than the groom himself. With the help of this book, as the day approaches, a gentleman can add to the joy, rather than the jitters. He may even give cause for amazement when the apprehensive spouse-to-be asks, "Now, where should the groomsmen go to pick up their rentals?" if he can calmly take a hand in his and say, "Don't worry, dear, I've already taken care of that."

There will be a moment of stunned astonishment, a pause, and then, almost simultaneously, they will look into each other's eyes and murmur, "I love you, more than you know."

Every wedding, after all, should begin as wonderfully as that.

A Toast to the Bride from the Groom, on Their Wedding Day

"Today is a day filled with miracles; the most magical of those miracles is you."

I.

THE MAIN MAN

The Groom

A gentleman never simply assumes that he is going to be married; he always asks the bride before making the announcement.

———————

Even if he is certain he has already won his loved one's heart, a gentleman remembers that a marriage proposal is best shared by two people, and two people only. A gentleman never catches a lady off guard.

———————

A gentleman always remembers that a wedding—like the marriage that follows it—is basically about two people, no matter how many other people get involved in the decision making.

———————

If a gentleman has never met his fiancée's parents, he at least makes their acquaintance before the wedding is announced.

A gentleman does not consider an e-mail message a proper introduction to his future in-laws, especially one that says, "Hey! Check me out on Facebook!!"

———

During the initial planning for the wedding, the groom and the bride-to-be work side by side. As the planning proceeds, however, he knows that he may sometimes be left on the sidelines.

———

When it comes to the actual wedding ceremony, the groom follows the instructions of the minister, priest, rabbi, judge, justice of the peace, or other officiant leading the ceremony.

Regarding arrangements for wedding parties, the flowers for the ceremony, or any matter related to the reception, unless the decision grates fiercely against his personal convictions, the groom quietly acquiesces to the wishes of the bride or the advice of the wedding planner.

———

If the wedding planner's advice grates fiercely against his personal convictions—or his hopes for the wedding day—the groom carries his concerns directly to the bride, since she and her family are most often the wedding planner's employers.

———

If the groom has concerns about the wedding plans, he expresses them as soon as possible and as clearly and directly as he can. (If the groom has *serious* concerns about the wedding plans, he does not say, "Okay, honey. Whatever you want.")

A gentlemanly groom knows that it is his job to add to the delight of the wedding day—not to its difficulty.

———

If a gentleman is not well acquainted with the parents of the bride-to-be, and until he is told to do otherwise, he addresses them as "Mr. and Mrs. Brown."

———

Once Mr. and Mrs. Brown say, "Call us Jerry and Marcia," a gentleman addresses them by their first names.

———

If Mr. and Mrs. Brown say, "Call us Mom and Dad," a gentleman does so—provided there are not already a "Mom and Dad" in his life. If such is the case, he feels free to say, "What about Jerry and Marcia?"

At the very least, as the planning for the wedding begins, the groom makes sure it is scheduled for a day that is open on his calendar. If said date is not open on the groom's calendar, he changes his calendar, unless he expects to be deployed to a war zone or is anticipating major surgery.

———

A gentleman understands that his wedding day will be unlike any other day in his life.

———

When planning their wedding, a gentleman and his spouse-to-be always talk about money—almost as soon as they talk about love.

TRADITIONAL DUTIES
OF THE GROOM

- Ask the bride to spend the rest of her life with him, in mutual, unalloyed bliss
- Pick out and present the engagement ring
- Ask the bride's father, her mother, or both her parents for her hand in marriage—if that is what the bride wishes him to do
- Introduce the bride to his own parents, if they have not met
- Introduce the bride's parents to his own parents
- Give his honest opinion as to the overall plans for the ceremony, especially if he and the bride are footing the bill
- Keep his opinions to himself otherwise, unless the wedding plans conflict with his moral convictions or fill him with unease
- Help pick out the wedding rings
- Select his best man, ushers, and groomsmen
- Plan and make arrangements for the honeymoon in collaboration with the bride, unless he has accepted the risk of planning the trip as a surprise
- Help develop the guest list
- Help his own mother understand that there are real limitations to the size of the guest list
- With cooperation from the bride and/or the best man, coordinate rental or purchase of formalwear or suits for his attendants

- Participate, gladly, in the process of registering for gifts
- Participate in pre-wedding parties, as requested or required
- Assist his own parents in planning for the rehearsal dinner
- Remember to obtain the wedding license
- Approve the plans for the bachelor party
- Make an appointment, well ahead of time, to get his hair cut—at least two days before the wedding
- Pick up his formalwear for the ceremony, well in advance, after trying it on at the shop, to make sure it fits
- Show up on time for the wedding rehearsal
- Attend the rehearsal dinner, prepared to make an appropriate toast
- Attend the bachelor party
- Arrive at the wedding ceremony on time
- Make sure the best man has the ring
- Participate in the ceremony, as directed by the officiant and/or the wedding planner
- Take his place in the receiving line at the reception, greeting guests and making introductions as necessary and appropriate
- Dance with the bride, his own mother, the mother of the bride, the maid of honor, and various bridesmaids
- Make sure to leave the reception in plenty of time to get to the airport or the hotel's honeymoon suite
- Do his part in writing the thank-you notes

What the Groom Traditionally Pays For

- The engagement ring
- The bride's wedding ring (she pays for his ring)
- His share of the bachelor party, if it involves travel (unless the members of his wedding party make it clear that he is traveling as their guest)
- The bride's bouquet (unless her parents insist on paying for all the flowers), as selected by the bride and designed by the florist of her choice
- Flowers for the mother of the bride and his mother, if they wish to wear them
- His own formalwear for the ceremony
- Ties and gloves for his attendants (unless they are included in the rental of their formalwear)
- A gift for the bride, presented to her, in private, after the rehearsal dinner
- A gift for the best man and for each of his ushers and groomsmen
- A thank-you gift for the minister, or other officiant at the ceremony
- All honeymoon expenses (unless the bride and he are sharing the costs)

Connubial Costs
Who Pays for What?

The days are long gone when it could automatically be assumed that the father of the bride would serve as Mr. Moneybags, covering every imaginable cost related to the wedding ceremony and the ensuing reception. If a father wishes to make such a commitment, that is his choice, of course. It is an offer that, in most cases, the bride and groom will gladly accept, the groom offering a handshake and saying, "Mr. Fierstein, you are very, very kind."

On the other hand, the couple may find themselves feeling more than a trifle uncomfortable with such a situation, perhaps because they have questions as to the frailty of the father's finances, or perhaps because they simply envision a simple celebration— or even an elaborate one—at which they will be serving as the hosts. Such is quite often the case when the bride and groom have already set up housekeeping, or when they are both already well embarked on their professional lives.

What's more, they may have good friends, or a well-meaning aunt or uncle, who wish to participate in making the magic happen. If such is the case, there is no reason the father of the bride should feel neglected, displaced, or affronted. Neither is it the business of any outsider to comment on the financing of the festivities.

It is essential, however, that all parties involved in the partying be clear as to how the expenses are being shared. Such matters are best handled up front and straightforwardly. For example, the couple may simply state, as graciously and lovingly as possible, "We're looking forward to throwing our own reception" or, "We hope you'll understand that we want this wedding to be our own gift to our friends."

Without breathing too obvious a sigh of relief, the father of the bride may respond by saying, "You are two wonderful people. Let's talk about the specifics as soon as we can. You know Mollie's mother and I want to be part of this wonderful moment, in whatever way you'd like us to be." Both he and the bride's mother will understand, of course, that it is the wedding of a new couple that is in the works—not a replay of their own nuptials from decades before.

If the couple is in charge of their own budget, however, it must be a budget they can readily handle. The groom, caught up in the potential romance of the moment, does not commit to more than he can logically afford to pay. Nothing could be more embarrassing, at the end of the day, than for him to find himself forced to approach the bride's father, much less his own, with a handful of overdue bills. He hopes to not establish a precedent he will inevitably come to resent as the years grow long. A gentleman understands that patterns set during the planning for a wedding are patterns laid for life.

If, however, it is the bride's parents who are underwriting every aspect of the wedding, the groom expects only to cover those expenses that are traditionally his own. If such is the situation, it is not his responsibility to worry about the bills. If he must vent, he shares his concerns privately with his best man, who, in the best of situations, is also his best friend.

When it comes to the seating at the wedding ceremony or the guest list for the reception, the gentleman asks his bride specifically how many invitations his family may send.

———————

When a gentleman asks how many invitations his family may send, he repeats the question, asking, "Does that mean Mom can send one hundred invitations, or does that mean that Mom can invite one hundred people to the ceremony?"

———————

When a gentleman gets a frank response to this question, he conveys the answer directly to his mother.

———————

If the gentleman's mother is not happy with this answer, he intervenes, as diplomatically as he possibly can, knowing all the while that it is the mother of the bride, as hostess for the ceremony, who has the ultimate word.

If his own mother is asked, as mother of the groom, to wear yellow, and even if she loathes yellow, the gentleman-groom says, "Mom, please wear yellow. It will just make life easier. Please do it for me."

————

If a gentleman does not own formal clothes, he rents them, reserving the suit well ahead of time.

————

If a gentleman expects to wear a bow tie at his wedding, he learns how to tie it—and practices tying it—well before the wedding day.

————

No matter how imaginative his bride may be, a gentleman always attempts to steer her away from lime green tuxedoes or color-coordinated wedding ensembles.

If a gentleman is given his preference as to the dress of his wedding party, he declares gray tailcoats for a prenoon wedding, "strollers" for an afternoon wedding, black-tie for an evening wedding, or white-tie for a ceremony commencing after 7 P.M. (For full details, please see chapter 5.)

THE BIG QUESTION

There can be no more important decision for a gentleman than choosing the moment when he will ask a lady to marry him. The moment may be highly dramatic, complete with a four-course dinner and the presentation of a diamond ring. Or it may come more quietly, during a walk on the beach. Either way, a gentleman knows that the timing must be right and that he must choose his words wisely. He must avoid any suggestion of "popping the question," as if he were only asking her to marry him as a brilliant, spur-of-the-moment inspiration.

Whether he has thought to bring roses and an engagement ring or whether his action is spontaneous, a gentleman says something like, "I've been thinking a lot about this lately—about you and me, and I want you to know how much, and how deeply, I love you. I want us to be married, and I'm hoping that you feel the same way too."

A gentleman makes sure the lady knows that he wants this, the most important decision of their lives, to be a mutual one, the beginning of a lifetime of shared decisions.

Five Things a Gentleman Does *Not* Say When Proposing Marriage

- "I've sown all my wild oats now, honey. So I guess it's time for me to settle down."
- "You know, sweetheart, neither of us is getting any younger."
- "Friends tell me I'm afraid of commitment, but I'm ready to try this with you."
- "I know you've been waiting a long time to hear this. So, will you marry me?"
- "I promise you, if you marry me now, you'll never regret it."

When proposing marriage, a gentleman refrains from talking about "settling down." He does not suggest any regret at putting his bachelor days behind him. The past is not the subject of the conversation at hand. The topic under discussion is the joy and excitement of a lifetime together, shared by two people in love.

―――――

A gentleman knows that it is not the cost of the ring that matters. What matters is that it makes the bride-to-be happy in the way he intends to make her happy, and that she loves it in the same way that she loves him.

Seven Essential Guidelines for Buying an Engagement Ring

1. A gentleman does his research before even considering the purchase of an engagement ring. Not only will it very likely be the most costly gift he has ever purchased; it is also a token of his devotion, one that his bride-to-be will treasure for the rest of her life. He will give it at least as much attention as he gives to shopping for a car.

2. As the time comes closer for buying the engagement ring, a gentleman listens and watches closely, in hopes that he will purchase a ring that is precisely the one she wants. If he still needs additional guidance (does she prefer yellow gold, platinum, or white gold?), he consults her friends, hoping they will keep the conversation in confidence.

3. A gentleman sets his budget before walking into the jewelry store. (Pre-shopping online may be helpful in this regard.) Buying a ring that costs four times as much as he can afford is not a demonstration of lifetime devotion. It is a guarantee of financial distress.

4. A gentleman buys from a reputable jeweler. If the price seems too good to be true, what looks like a first-class diamond may well turn out to be a cubic zirconia. A reputable jeweler will appreciate a gentleman's asking

questions about cut, color, clarity, and carat weight, known as the "4 C's of diamond buying."

5. If a gentleman is convinced that a family-heirloom diamond is the stone he wishes his intended to wear, he presents it proudly, saying, "My great-grandfather gave this diamond to my great-grandmother on their 50th wedding anniversary. I hope we can pick out the setting together."

6. A gentleman does his best to determine his bride's correct ring size, recognizing full well that the bride herself may not know what size she wears. He asks for the jeweler's guidance in purchasing a ring that is of a medium size. If it turns out to be too large or too small, the gentleman immediately reassures the bride-to-be, saying, "We're going together, tomorrow, to have it resized."

7. A gentleman purchases insurance for the engagement ring. The bride-to-be may insist that she will never take it off. But she will.

Classic Cuts of Diamonds for an Engagement Ring

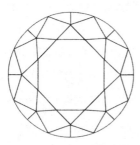

Round

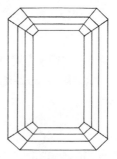

Emerald

Marquise

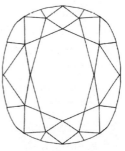

Cushion

Heart

A gentleman knows that the presentation of an engagement ring is not a laughing matter. A diamond ring hidden in a scoop of frozen yogurt may seem amusing in theory. A chipped tooth and a trip to the oral surgeon can rip the romance out of any gesture.

Six Things a Gentleman Does *Not* Say When Presenting an Engagement Ring

- "I know it's not much, but it's all I could afford."
- "There's a tiny flaw in it, but the jeweler promised me nobody could see it."
- "Hope you know we're gonna eat a lot of ramen noodles before this thing gets paid off."
- "If this doesn't prove how much I love you, nothing will."
- "You better not lose this."
- "Is it okay?"

If a groom and his bride have decided to elope, they make sure they are well-informed as to the laws regarding marriage at their wedding destination.

A gentleman and his bride do not worry about defending their decision to elope. Instead, they simply say, "For us, it was the right thing to do."

———

A gentleman does not brag about how much money he saved by opting for an elopement. Neither does he talk about the size of the check he received from the grateful father of the bride.

———

Friends of the bride and groom never assume that an elopement implies a "shotgun wedding."

———

A gentleman knows that the decision to elope is one that must be mutual. He would never attempt to deprive his bride-to-be of the wedding of her dreams.

Project Runaway

It is entirely possible that a gentleman and his lady love may decide to avoid all the expense and potential anxiety of planning a full-scale wedding ceremony. What's more, they may wish to proceed as expeditiously as possible to start their married life. If such is their wish, they may choose to slip quietly away to the courthouse, a minister's study, or the chambers of a friendly judge. Provided that plans for the wedding ceremony are not already under way (with nonrefundable deposits already in the hands of the caterer and the bridesmaids already fitted for their dresses), the bride and groom need not announce their decision to anyone. Nevertheless, once they have signed the marriage certificate, they will be well-advised to inform their parents and their best friends as soon as possible.

Such announcements may be sent through the mail, just as formal wedding invitations would be, or the couple may depend on a newspaper announcement as their means of spreading the word. The couple may also register for gifts, just as they would have done before a full-scale wedding. Friends may wish to celebrate their nuptials with after-the-fact parties. The reason for rejoicing remains the same.

In some cases, only half-jokingly, the father of the bride may suggest, "Why don't all of us just go to the preacher (or to the courthouse, or to Vegas), and keep this whole thing as simple as possible. Then I can just write you a check, you can have a wonderful trip, and you can get started on your lovely life together." The gentleman may wish to say, "Sounds like a good idea to me," but he will be wise to let the lady make her own half-joking response, which will probably be, "Oh, Daddy, you are too, too funny"; "Oh, Daddy, you know I've always dreamed of a wonderful wedding"; or, more likely, "Oh, Daddy, you know that Mother would *kill* us—you, me, *and* Bill."

If the bride-to-be makes it clear that she wishes to use her own name after the wedding, the groom-to-be graciously accepts her decision.
If he is uncomfortable with the decision, he tells her so, knowing full well that the choice is still ultimately her own.

———————

Should friends or family members question the bride's decision to use her own name, the groom replies, as simply as possible, "That's Gloria's and my choice. Hope we'll see you at the wedding."

Life with Father,
and/or Mother

A Time Honored Tradition: Asking
for Her Hand in Marriage

Once it is clear that the lady shares the gentleman's feelings and that she is actually pleased by the prospect of the two of them spending their lives together, the gentleman may wish to approach her father and/or her mother and "ask for her hand in marriage." Age-old and underused though this tradition might be, there may be wisdom in honoring it—especially in a case where the gentleman and the lady's parents are not well acquainted.

It is the gentleman's responsibility to set up the appointment. If he is fully confident that his request will be met with ready approval, he may invite either, or both, of the lady's parents to lunch or for a drink in a quiet restaurant; the better option in any case is for the gentleman to simply call the lady's father and say, "Mr. Fromley, I was wondering if I might stop by and have a chat with you tomorrow evening. There's something very important, and very positive, I'd like to discuss with you." He never arranges this meeting at the father's office—unless that is what the father insists upon—and he never, ever says, "I'd like us to get together; I've got a little business I'd like us to discuss."

When asking for a lady's hand, the gentleman makes it clear that he and his intended have already discussed the matter and that they both look forward to their wedding day. If the lady's father is not entirely pleased with the prospect of having this particular gentleman as his son-in-law, he states his misgivings in as direct and kind spirited a manner as possible. Nevertheless, the days are pretty much gone when the lady's father is likely to reply with a threat to "cut her off without a penny." His best response is to say, "Let me share this news with Stephanie's mother; I'm sure Stephanie and she have already talked about it, of course. You know how precious she is to both of us; we wish you all the best of everything."

Shortly thereafter, the gentleman will probably receive a call from the lady's mother, expressing her happiness at the good news. In the same conversation, she will probably laugh and ask, "Have the two of you talked about a date? You know we've got a wedding to plan."

It is entirely possible that, when it comes to asking for the lady's hand in marriage, the groom may find himself making that request to the lady's mother—either because she is widowed or because the lady's parents are divorced and her father has little involvement in her life. In that case, the gentleman proceeds exactly as he would if he were asking for the approval of the lady's father—being even more careful to avoid any hint of setting up a "business transaction."

The lady may request, however, that the gentleman not ask for the approval of her parents, saying, "This is our decision, George. I love my parents, but let's just get together with them, the two of us, and tell them the good news." If such is her wish, he honors her request readily and probably with a sigh of relief.

Seize the Day

Finding the Perfect Day for the Perfect Wedding

Once it has been decided that there will actually *be* a wedding, a gentleman and his bride-to-be must face the challenge of deciding when and where that wedding will take place. Almost invariably, that decision will not be entirely in their own hands.

Certainly, they will start by considering their individual work schedules and upcoming holiday seasons, but their decision may also be driven by the availability of the house of worship, the hotel ballroom, or the public garden that is the venue of choice for their dream wedding. If they are wise, they will seek the input of their parents—especially the bride's parents, who may very well be footing the bill for the entire celebration. Even if the couple are picking up the tab themselves, they will be thoughtful to make sure that all parents who may wish to be involved will at least be in the country on the day of the wedding. In the end, the choice of the wedding day may depend on the availability of a certain caterer or a particular florist, the travel schedule of the best man or maid of honor,

or the date by which the wedding dress can
be finished.

A gentleman understands that this
is but the first step in what may well be
a convoluted series of conversations,
negotiations, and congenial compromises.
He does not wait until the bride has fixed on
a particular date, however, before offering
his own suggestions—which may relate to
his work schedule or the planning for the
honeymoon. He may even wish to begin
the dialogue himself as soon as possible
after he has presented the diamond, bravely
plunging in and saying, "Honey, this is going
to be wonderful. Shouldn't we go ahead and
set the date? I've got the most spectacular
honeymoon in mind."

Friends of Choice

When a gentleman chooses the gentlemen who will stand alongside him on his wedding day, he turns to the friends who have stood by him through the happiest times in his life—and the toughest times too. He understands that in asking a friend to serve as his best man, as an usher, or as a groomsman, he is paying that friend a compliment, but he is also asking that friend to assume certain responsibilities as well.

If the groom-to-be has brothers, it is traditional for him to ask them to join his wedding party. He will most likely invite his oldest brother, if he has more than one, to serve as his best man, and ask his other brothers to serve as ushers or groomsmen. The groom may even ask his own father to stand next to him at the altar. If the groom-to-be has a long-term best friend, however, he may feel perfectly comfortable asking that friend to serve as his best man. To avoid any possibility that his family members will feel slighted, he informs them of his decision as soon as possible, saying, "Hank, I'm asking Tom to serve as my best man. I hope you'll be one of my groomsmen." He need offer no explanation as to why he has asked Hank to serve as his best man, and, provided they are on good terms with their brother, his siblings have no reason to feel slighted by his decision.

The number of attendants in his wedding party is determined by the number of women the bride includes in her party. Usually, the groom-to-be includes one gentleman attendant to escort each of the bridesmaids. (The best man escorts the maid- or matron of honor, of course.) If a groom wishes to include additional friends in his contingent, he may ask them to serve as ushers, assisting in the seating of guests but not in the actual ceremony. Or they may walk down the aisle, side by side, during both the processional and the recessional.

A gentleman may wish to include friends who have previously included him in their own wedding parties, understanding the bride has no obligation to include their spouses among her attendants.

When inviting a friend to join his wedding party, a gentleman must remember that he is asking his friend to make a commitment of time as well as money. If his family, or the bride's family, can afford it, they cover the cost of travel and lodging for the best man and the groom's other attendants. Many of the meals for the groom's attendants will usually be taken care of in the form of parties and receptions. The parents may also pick up the tab for the rental of formalwear.

Frequently, especially if the gentlemen are already embarked on their professional careers, the members of the groom's party will be expected to pay their own way, in full. What's more, each will be expected to pay his own share of the bachelor-party expenses, as well as his share of a gift for the groom, and the cost of a gift for the fortunate couple. A gentleman remembers those realities as he begins selecting his attendants, since they will usually feel obligated to accept the honor inherent in his request.

He does not take it upon himself to assess his friends' financial statuses, but he attempts not to put an undue stress on others, or to put them in awkward situations. If the end result is that he has fewer groomsmen than the bride has bridesmaids, she may arrange the entry and departure of her attendants in a way that compensates for the unequal numbers.

With This Ring . . .

In many cases, the groom may wish to surprise his bride-to-be when presenting her with her engagement ring, but the choice of the couple's wedding rings is a joint decision. Since the groom is expected to pay for the bride's ring, and she is expected to pay for his, the selection will be determined by their individual budgets—and by their personal tastes. The rings are usually identical in design, whether they are purchased from a commercial jeweler or handcrafted by a specially commissioned artisan.

If it is at all possible, the bride and groom should go shopping for their wedding rings together. They may exchange ideas, sketches, and catalog images via the Internet, but they are well-advised to try on the rings, in person and together, and to make sure they are properly fitted, before the day of the wedding.

In order to prevent unwanted clumsiness and awkward moments, they may even wish to practice slipping them on each other's ring fingers.

"Altar-cations"
CHOOSING THE OFFICIANT OF CHOICE

If the bride and groom are active, or even semi-active, members of a church, a synagogue, or any other sort of religious community, they may have little problem selecting the minister who will conduct their wedding ceremony. If they have no religious affiliation, or if they are of different faiths, however, selecting a minister may leave them in a quandary.

If they are to be married in a church, a synagogue, or another house of worship, they will most often be expected to be married by a minister of that faith. At the very least, it will be expected that a minister of that faith participate in the ceremony. In such cases, as soon as they have decided to be married, they will be wise to begin asking friends or relations for recommendations. Logically, they will want to make the minister's acquaintance before the day of the ceremony. The minister may also require that they participate in prenuptial counseling before he or she agrees to lead the ceremony.

If the bride and groom are to be married in a private home, a public garden, or a hotel ballroom, however, they may wish to opt for a civil ceremony, with a justice of the peace, a judge, or some other public official doing the honors. At any rate, if they are to enjoy the legal benefits of marriage, some government-sanctioned person must say the words and sign the papers that pronounce them husband and wife.

In many states and municipalities, a friend or relative of the couple may be granted short-term permission to conduct a civil marriage ceremony. The bride and groom will be wise to consult a local government office—the office of the mayor, a judge, or perhaps the chief of police—before proceeding on that assumption, of course.

If the bride and groom are not of the same faith, or if one is religious and the other is not, it will be wise for them to discuss religion-related matters well before they begin plans for the wedding ceremony.

If a gentleman and his bride-to-be choose to write their own vows, they plan them well ahead of time.

————

If a gentleman and his bride-to-be are of a singularly sentimental bent, they may wish to read their self-written vows to each other, at least eight hours before the ceremony itself. They have no desire to be surprised at that moment.

————

In the rehearsal reading, the gentleman and his bride-to-be do not critique each other's vows. They listen and say, "I love you." Then one or the other of them may whisper, "Can I get a copy for my files?"

A gentleman knows that a wedding ceremony, in front of one hundred friends and well-wishers, is no occasion for surprise, shock, or uncontrollable outbursts of tears—no matter how much the one hundred friends and well-wishers may long for them.

————

If a gentleman has composed his own wedding vows, he writes them down. He does not assume that he will be able to keep them in his memory at the actual ceremony. Therefore, he keeps them at his fingertips.

————

A gentleman prints out his self-composed wedding vows on stiff card stock and grips them tightly. He does not trust fragile copy paper, which will shake because his hands will be shaking too.

A gentleman shares a copy of his wedding vows with his best man, since it is likely he will be unable to locate his own copy once he is in the midst of the actual ceremony.

———

If a gentleman and his bride are to be married in a house of worship where there is a structured liturgy, and unless the minister-in-charge allows otherwise, they read the vows that are set before them, looking lovingly into each other's eyes all the while.

———

A gentleman does not invent his own marriage vows on the spot. He drafts them out, several days before the ceremony. He writes them down. He practices them, in the privacy of his own room—perhaps in the presence of a good friend, such as his best man.

People-ing the Pews

Once the couple have announced their plans to marry—and even before they have set the date, secured a site for the ceremony, and selected the officiant who will pronounce them man and wife—they will encounter one of the most daunting challenges they will ever face in their life together. They must develop the guest list.

Since the bride's parents usually cover the costs of the wedding and the reception, it is their privilege, and their challenge, to decide who receives the majority of the invitations. If the bride's mother is thoughtful at all, however, she will contact the groom's mother, stating clearly, but graciously, how many invitations are available for the groom's family's friends and relations. Depending on the size of the ceremony, and the reception following it, she may say, "We hope you'll want to invite 75 people [or 25, or 250]. I'm hoping we can have the guest list in hand by April 1 [or September 15, or whenever]."

From the very beginning, the groom does his best to make sure everyone in his family understands that "75 people" actually means 75 *people*. It does not mean 75 *invitations*, since any one invitation might actually be adding two, or even more, people to the guest list.

It is then the groom's responsibility to help make sure his mother sticks to the game plan, developing a guest list that stays within the boundaries suggested by the bride's family, and getting the list to the bride's mother by the requested deadline. To get the job done, and to get it done on time, without too many hurt feelings or bruised egos, he may find himself putting his best diplomatic skills to work.

The groom has an obvious right to take part in the creation of the list, consulting with the bride to make sure they have included as many as possible of their friends in common. But he also tries to include family members (at least those with whom he and his parents keep in contact with any regularity), his parents' closest friends, and his own personal friends as well. He does not invite his coworkers unless he also counts them as friends outside the office. And he never simply posts a copy of the invitation on the bulletin board in the office break room, with a "Hope you can all make it!" note attached.

If the ceremony is an intimate one, staged at home or in a small chapel, both the bride and the groom may limit their guest lists to their closest family members and their dearest friends. No matter what the limits are on the size of the congregation at the ceremony, additional guests may be invited for the reception that ensues.

If the ceremony is extremely private, with only family members included, the bride and groom may simply wish to send out announcements—letting all their friends and acquaintances know that the wedding has taken place, when and where it happened, and what the couple's home address will be.

It is extremely bad form for anyone to ask the groom (or the bride) why he or she has not been included on the guest list. Nevertheless, some particularly self-centered acquaintance may be rude enough to corner the groom, pressuring the poor fellow to know why he or she did not make the cut. In such an ungainly moment, the groom simply says, "Thank you for wanting to be there, Floyd [or Florence]. The list isn't as long as either Millicent or I would have wanted it to be. I wish you could be there too. Maybe we can get together and look at the photos after the honeymoon."

Picture-Perfect

Every bride and groom—and most particularly, every bride and her mother—will want a photographic record of the wedding day. No matter what anybody may tell the groom, simple snapshots will probably not be an alternative.

Tradition holds that the groom must not see the bride on their wedding day until she floats down the aisle, wearing a dress she has dreamed of all her life. Thus, wedding photos are often taken immediately after the ceremony, as soon as the guests have departed for the reception.

It is not unusual today, however, for the wedding party to gather in the church an hour or so before the ceremony to pose for their formal portraits. In some instances, the wedding photos may even have been shot earlier in the day, perhaps in a public garden or in some handsome historic building. In that case, the groom makes sure that the members of his wedding party are aware of the schedule, so they can show up on time and not delay the picture-taking process.

Despite the advent of digital cameras, picture-taking and video-recording simply are not permitted in many historic houses of worship—especially during wedding ceremonies or worship services. No matter what the official rules are, though, the whirring of cameras or the presence of scurrying amateur videographers is likely to prove a distraction and an intrusion on what is meant to be a solemn, albeit happy, moment. If the groom-to-be gets wind of the fact that a well-meaning friend or relation plans to bring along his own camera equipment, the groom will be wise to say, "That's swell of you, Uncle Bob, but I'm afraid they don't allow picture-taking during ceremonies at First Lutheran," or "That's thoughtful of you, Uncle Joe, but Millicent and I are asking that there be no photos during the ceremony. Hope you'll bring your camera to the reception, though."

A gentleman always writes his share
of the thank-you notes.

———————

A gentleman writes his thank-you notes
by hand, using black or blue-black ink,
using clear cursive script.

———————

If he cannot write in clear cursive
script, a gentleman writes his thank-you
notes in box print, or however
clearly he can.

———————

Even if a gentleman cannot write clearly,
he still writes his thank-you notes by
hand, trusting that, at the end of his
scrambling, the words "Thank you" will
still be clear at the end.

Thank You Very Much

If a gentleman has any input at all into the guest list for the wedding, he also takes responsibility for saying thank you for the gifts that arrive in response to the wedding invitations. If most of his friends and family members are from out of town, the bride may find herself receiving gifts from people she has never met, or scarcely heard of. In such cases, unless the bride insists on writing every thank-you note herself, a gentleman gladly volunteers to do the honors.

What's more, the bride and groom may in fact have collaborated in selecting the wish list of gifts "registered" at various stores or on various Web sites. Not all wedding gifts have to be china, glassware, or kitchen gadgets, and many gifts may have been selected with the groom, as well as the bride, in mind. If the bride and groom are the outdoors type, for instance, they may wish to steer their friends toward a sporting goods store; if they are avid readers, they may suggest that their friends visit a favorite bookstore; if they are wine lovers, they may suggest a wine store where the staff is familiar with their favorite vintages. A particularly generous group of friends, maybe even the members of the wedding party, may go together to purchase tickets for the football season or the symphony series.

In such cases, a gentleman may take the lead in saying thank you, or he and the bride may both write a couple of lines of gratitude on the same thank-you note. Or he may, at the very least, add at the bottom of the note, "Thanks so much. We both love the toaster. Joe."

He does his best, no matter what, to pay attention as the gifts begin to arrive, so that when he runs into a generous friend, he can say, "Georgette, you were so kind to send us the afghan. It will help us plan the colors for our living room."

A gentleman knows that a thank-you note need not be elaborate or self-consciously eloquent. He keeps it simple, making sure to mention the gift itself and how much he and the bride will enjoy using it. He does his best, however, to do his part in the job of note-writing, so the thank-yous go out as quickly as possible, whether the gift is received before or after the wedding.

A Thank-You Note for a Wedding Gift
Received Before the Wedding

Dear Aunt Millicent,

You were so kind to send us the wonderful bottles of balsamic vinegar. Patricia and I both love spending time in the kitchen; in fact, one of our first dates was a gourmet cooking class. We'll whip up some tasty vinaigrettes, I know, thanks to you.

We both look forward to seeing you on the 17th.

Much love,
Jack

A Thank-You Note for a Wedding Gift
Received After the Wedding

Dear Bill and Larry,

Patricia and I are just back from Barbados, so we've just opened the great set of monogrammed golf tees. (Very clever how you managed to work in all our initials.) Every time we use them, on sunshiny days on the course, we'll think of you. Let's get together for a drink some time soon. We promise not to bore you too much with the honeymoon pictures.

Thanks, and all best,
Jack

Just Between the Two of Us . . .

Traditionally, at some private moment, when no one else is watching and there is a pause in the pre-ceremony celebrations, the groom presents the bride with his own wedding gift to her. (There could not be a more perfect moment than the evening of the wedding rehearsal.)

The gift need not be expensive; but it must be exquisitely well chosen, a gift that demonstrates his understanding of her and his affection for her. This may, in fact, be the perfect moment for him to present her with the brooch his grandfather gave his grandmother or the string of pearls she will pass along to her own granddaughters. It is the gift she will be showing to her own grandchildren, decades hence, growing a bit misty-eyed when she says, "Your grandfather gave me these pearls on the day we were married, 57 years ago. Saying 'I do,' standing up there alongside him, is the most wonderful thing I've ever done."

Five Gifts a Gentleman Does *Not* Present to the Bride on the Eve of Their Wedding

1. A blender, mixer, can opener, food processor, or any other item that might remotely remind her of the kitchen
2. A vacuum cleaner
3. A gym membership
4. Her own handgun
5. A big-screen television or any other gift that the gentleman actually wants for himself

The Folks at Home

As soon as it is clear that he and the love of his life are to be married, the gentleman makes every effort to inform his own parents of that decision. The last thing he wants is for such news to be overheard as if it were gossip. And the very last place he wants his own mother to hear the news is from the mother of the bride-to-be. A little forethought forestalls bruised feelings. What's more, it shows the gentleman's parents the respect and deference that are their due.

Party, Party, Party

Once it has been announced, both among friends and family and to the general public, that a wedding is in the offing, a flurry of parties is likely to begin. The celebrating may break out with an engagement party, hosted by the bride's parents. On the other hand, if the bride- and groom-to-be have both begun their professional careers—or if the couple already live together—they may wish to throw their own announcement party, so they can share the good news with their best friends. Well-meaning and good-hearted though it may be, the sequence of celebrations can threaten to grow exhausting.

The groom may feel fortunate not to have to attend every event on the agenda. He will not be expected to participate in the bride's showers or the bridesmaids' luncheon, for example. But he will be called upon to participate, graciously and happily, in any parties planned in honor of him *and* the bride. For instance, a group of friends may go together to host a "Stock the Kitchen/Fill the Toolbox" party, a "Trim-the-Tree" party, or a "Stock the Bar" shower. In such cases, the groom does his best to add to the joy of the occasion, making sure to express his gratitude to the hosts at the end of the evening, and doing his part in writing the thank-you notes—beginning the next day.

He is duly obligated, of course, to participate in his own bachelor dinner, the rehearsal dinner, and the wedding reception. If he finds himself balking at the prospect of any of these parties, he may want to reconsider the prospect of a swift, less-complicated elopement.

At a Distance
DESTINATION WEDDINGS

While the spouses-to-be may dream
of a wedding on an exotic isle or in the
courtyard of a castle in Scotland, they must
surely understand that participating in such
"destination weddings" places a heavy
burden—budget-wise, schedule-wise, and
otherwise—on the invited guests.

An overlong invitation list for this sort
of celebration borders on poor taste. It
is impolite to taunt good friends with the
temptations of a party they will be unlikely
to attend. It is also impolite to suggest that
people spend more money than they may
have on hand, at one's own behest.

Such weddings, appropriately, take on
the spirit of intimate, at-home celebrations,
despite the fact that they are happening
on the other side of the country, much
less on the other side of the globe. Only a
few friends are likely to be there, so only a
reasonable number of friends are invited.

The rest of the couple's friends and
acquaintances are notified about the
ceremony after it has occurred, via a formal
wedding announcement, sent via standard
mail. (E-mail is not good enough, if the
friends are good friends at all.) Since they

have not been invited to the wedding, and certainly not to the reception, those friends are under no duress to give gifts. They will nevertheless send gifts along, no matter what, so the bride and groom need feel no fear for lack of china and flatware.

Remote weddings may, however, pose a particular challenge for the groom's wedding party, and for his closest friends, especially if the "bachelor party" also takes the form of a weekend bacchanalia in a major city or at a tropical resort. If the friend—even if he is a groomsman—cannot afford to participate in both events, he opts for the wedding. What other choice could there be?

In Gratitude

During the planning for the wedding ceremony, or in its wake, a gentlemanly groom may wish to say thank you for any number of kindnesses. He may specifically wish to say thank you to his friends who have agreed to stand up with him at the altar—or he may wish to thank the bride's parents for giving him the great love of his life.

A Thank-You Note to the Best Man
(perhaps included with a gift from the groom)

Dear Terrance,

When we met at that pick-up ball game our freshman year at OSU, I knew I'd met one of the greatest guys in the world. I remember how hard we laughed that night as we headed back to the dorm. We've done a lot of laughing since, but we've stuck with each other through some tough times too. Thank you for agreeing to stand alongside me tomorrow evening, just as you've been standing by me all these years.

All my best,
Ralph

A Thank-You Note to a Groomsman or Usher
(perhaps included with a gift from the groom)

Dear Barry,

 Tomorrow evening will be a happy time for Margie and me. But it will be even happier because of your being a part of it.

 Thanks for standing up there with me on the most important evening of my life.

All my best,
Ralph

A Note to the Father and/or Mother of the Bride
(upon the bride and groom's decision to marry)

Dear Mr. and Mrs. Goodman [or Mr. Goodman, or Mrs. Goodman],

 I hope you know that you have given me the greatest gift in the world. I promise that I will do everything in my power to make Margie happy and to support her, wherever her wonderful spirit takes her.

 Thank you for letting me be a part of her life—and for letting me be a part of your lives too.

Sincerely,
Ralph Thorne

By Way of Acknowledgment
The Groom's Gifts to His Friends

In gratitude for their friendship and in acknowledgment of their generosity in serving as members of his wedding party, the groom provides a gift for each of his attendants. He may choose to present them all at the same time—the bachelor party offers a convenient opportunity (although gift-giving may prove awkward if friends who are not attendants are present), as does a brief backstage gathering before the ceremony. If his schedule allows, however, the groom may wish to present each gift in private, thanking each friend individually for taking part in his wedding.

Unless he is particularly inventive and intimately acquainted with the likes and dislikes of each of his friends, a gentleman will be well-advised to stick with identical gifts for all his attendants. However, the groom may choose to personalize them, monogramming each one with that attendant's initials.

The groom's gifts are intended as mementos of the wedding, so they need not be especially extravagant or costly. The gift will be most appreciated, however, if it is something his friends will actually *use*—a set of double old-fashioned glasses, perhaps, or a money clip, a set of cuff links, or a bottle of good whiskey, provided there are no teetotalers in the group.

"Snap" Shot

Near the close of the wedding reception, the groom may kneel before the bride and, ever so tastefully and gently, remove the garter from her right leg. The maneuver never comes as a surprise to the bride, of course, and has been carefully scripted into the agenda for the evening. (Should the bride be uncomfortable with this ritual, it may be ignored altogether.)

As the couple leaves the party, and just after she has tossed her bouquet to the ladies in the assemblage, he tosses the garter to the gentlemen at the gathering. (He does not snap it or make any gestures that summon up images of a college panty raid.) Although the removing of the garter once carried suggestions of the groom's "ownership" of the bride, the tossing of it now suggests a lighthearted farewell to his bachelor life and a hearty good wish to the next fellow who finds a bride as wondrous as his own.

Two for the Road

It is the groom's responsibility to pay for the
honeymoon, and it is also his job to make all the
travel arrangements. But, unless he is extremely
self-confident and fully convinced that he knows
the likes and dislikes of the bride-to-be, he
consults her on virtually every detail of the trip.
A few surprises during the wedding trip may add
to the fun and romance of the experience, but a
groom who attempts to keep the very nature of the
honeymoon—including the destination—a secret
is surely making trouble for himself, since he only
adds to the stress of the wedding planning, not to
mention the wedding day.

In many cases these days, the bride and groom
may set up a honeymoon savings account, to which
they both make contributions, so that the trip can
be everything they would like it to be. Likewise, the
bride's parents, the groom's parents, other relatives, or
even members of the wedding party may wish to help
cover the costs of the trip.

As planning for the trip gets under way, however,
the groom sets his own budget—or he and the bride
set it together. And they stick to it. The last thing
they will need when they return home to begin their
married life is a pile of un-payable credit card bills.

The bride will probably give considerable
attention to her wardrobe for the wedding trip,
but the groom may wish to think about his own
"trousseau" as well, using the honeymoon as an

excuse to purchase some new vacation clothes, a new sports coat, or a new ski jacket. Just as the bride will give some thought to her lingerie for the trip, he will treat himself to a fresh supply of undershirts and undershorts.

LEST WE FORGET . . .

A Groom's Guide to Classic Gifts for the Milestone Wedding Anniversaries

Anniversary	Traditional	Modern
1st	Paper	Clocks
2nd	Cotton	China
3rd	Leather	Crystal, Glass
4th	Linen, Silk	Appliances (electrical)
5th	Wood	Silverware
6th	Iron	Wood
7th	Wool, Copper	Desk/Pen and Pencil Sets
8th	Bronze	Linens, Lace
9th	Pottery, China	Leather
10th	Tin, Aluminum	Diamond Jewelry
11th	Steel	Fashion Jewelry, Accessories
12th	Silk	Pearls, Colored Gems
13th	Lace	Textiles, Furs
14th	Ivory	Gold Jewelry
15th	Crystal	Watches

Anniversary	Traditional	Modern
16th	Tourmaline	Silver Hollowware
17th	Furniture	Furniture
18th	Turquoise	Porcelain
19th	Aquamarine	Bronze
20th	China	Platinum
25th	Silver	Silver
30th	Pearl	Diamond
35th	Coral, Jade	Jade
40th	Ruby	Ruby
45th	Sapphire	Sapphire
50th	Gold	Gold
55th	Emerald	Emerald
60th	Yellow Diamond	Diamond
65th	Blue Sapphire	Star Sapphire
75th	Diamond	Diamond

(NB: Diamonds are never wrong.)

A gentleman remembers that—in
the minds of the general public,
and especially in the minds of
her parents—the wedding day is
always the bride's day. He does not
attempt to contradict that fact.

———

Even if he feels a bit neglected
on the wedding day, a gentleman
knows that he and the bride have a
lifetime to spend together.

II.

THE SUPPORTING CAST

The Best Man, Ushers and Groomsmen, and Even the Ring Bearer

SERGEANT AT ARMS:
THE BEST MAN

When a gentleman is asked to serve as best man at a friend's wedding, he knows he is being offered one of the highest honors one friend can bestow on another.

————

A gentleman does not dawdle when responding to the request to serve as a friend's best man. Neither does he waste any time in declining, should that be the case.

————

A gentleman understands that the title of best man is not merely an honorific. He recognizes that it comes with an actual job description, as well as a considerable commitment of time and other resources. For that reason, he thinks long and hard (but not too long) before giving his answer.

A gentleman does not accept this sort of signal honor via e-mail, a text message, or a posting on any sort of social networking system. Instead, he makes a phone call to the groom.

———

The best man accepts the groom's invitation by saying, "Ted, this is the nicest honor any guy could have. Let's get together soon, so you can give me all the plans." He does not neglect to add, "Please give Gloria all my love."

———

As soon as possible, upon accepting the job of best man, a gentleman takes the bride and groom to dinner or drinks—just the three of them—not only to congratulate them, but also to get a clear picture of their understanding of the best man's role in the upcoming celebrations.

When a gentleman accepts the honor of serving as best man, he also accepts all the realities that accompany the job—including the parties, the photo sessions, and the price tag.

———

A gentleman trusts his best man at all times as his backup—except for when he is saying, "I do."

———

If the best man organizes a golf game for the wedding day, he keeps careful watch over the groom, making sure he wears sunscreen, limits his alcohol intake, and allows ample time for shaving, showering, and dressing before departing for the ceremony or the photo session.

Traditional Duties of the Best Man

- Assist in coordinating and pickup of formalwear rentals for the groom's attendants
- Supervise planning for the bachelor party, helping to coordinate travel arrangements if it involves an out-of-town trip
- Attend the engagement party, as well as other parties and showers, as his schedule permits
- Assure the groom's safe arrival at the bachelor party and his safe return from it
- Participate in the wedding rehearsal
- Participate in the rehearsal dinner, serving as master of ceremonies if requested
- Offer a toast to the bride and groom at the rehearsal dinner
- Help organize activities for the groom's attendants on the day of the ceremony
- Stay at the groom's side, as much as possible, on the day of the ceremony
- Show up on time, properly dressed, for any photo shoots
- Make sure the groom is properly dressed
- Show up well ahead of time for the wedding ceremony (at least an hour before the scheduled starting time), with the groom in tow
- Take responsibility for the bride's ring on the day of the ceremony
- Serve as legal witness to the marriage, proudly signing the marriage certificate

- Participate in the wedding reception, mingling with guests and dancing with as many ladies from the bridal party as possible
- Offer a toast to the bride and groom and announce their first dance as husband and wife
- Keep watch over the groom's car and luggage to prevent any prankster-ish mayhem
- Discourage prankster-ish mayhem on the part of anyone—including members of the wedding party, members of the bride or groom's family, or high-spirited lifelong friends
- Coordinate return of his fellow attendants' formalwear

What the Best Man Traditionally Pays For

- His own travel expenses and lodging related to the wedding ceremony and other wedding-related events—unless the groom or one of the families offers to assist in covering those costs
- Rental of his own formalwear, or, if necessary, the purchase of other appropriate attire
- His fair share of the cost of a gift to the groom from all his attendants
- A gift for the bride and groom

To Stand, or Not to Stand
Will I be the Best Man, or Won't I?

A gentleman readily accepts the invitation to serve
as best man if he can possibly do so. Nevertheless,
he may decline the invitation for a number of
legitimate reasons: His schedule may not permit the
time commitment. (This may be especially true if he
lives out of town.) His budget may not allow for the
financial commitment. He may not feel that he is a
close enough friend of the groom. One of his close
relations may be in poor health. Or he simply may
not approve of the union. If he feels he must decline
the groom's kind offer, he says, "Ted, you are great to
think of me, but I'm going to have to say no. Please
know that I'm wishing you and Gloria all the best."

Should the groom apply pressure by asking,
"Why not?" or by attempting to negotiate, the
friend says, "I truly wish I could do this, Ted, but my
schedule at the office is just so unpredictable," or,
"You're great to ask me, Gus, but, as you know, Dad's
health is touch-and-go." He always adds, "This is
truly a great honor. But you need someone you can
absolutely depend on; right now, I fear that's not me."

Should the gentleman actually be declining
because he disapproves of the marriage, he
finds a legitimate excuse, such as travel plans or
responsibilities at work. He does not moralize or
preach, lest he lose a friend, or maybe two. He simply
sticks to his explanation.

If a gentleman is asked to serve as a groomsman as a default after being asked to serve as best man, he sticks with his original explanations. If his schedule and finances allow him to serve as a groomsman, he does so. If he is uncertain about the prospects for the marriage, he declines all invitations to join the wedding party without further comment.

Five Things a Gentleman Does *Not* Say When He's Asked to Serve as Best Man:

- "How much is this going to cost me?"
- "What do the bridesmaids look like?"
- "No way I can do this. Don't you remember I dated Stephanie, before you ever met her?"
- "Will I have to wear a tux?"
- "What's the problem? Did Sam and Jack turn you down first?"

The Only Two Responses a Gentleman May Offer When He's Asked to Serve as Best Man:

- "Thanks so much, Hank. I'm honored. It's a tall order, so let's get together soon. I want to be the best best man possible."
- "This is a great honor, Hank, but I fear I'm unable to accept it." At this point a gentleman will do well to insert some simple, straightforward explanation such as job

obligations; the illness of a family member; or pre-existing, unchangeable travel plans. (He does not say, "I probably just can't afford it.") In any case, he always adds, "Will you please give Phyllis my best, and all my love?"

As a gesture of respect and affection, a gentleman may ask his father to serve as his best man, standing alongside him, just as he has stood alongside him since the day of the bridegroom's birth. In such cases, however, the father of the groom will probably not be expected to organize the bachelor party. The rehearsal dinner remains his primary line of responsibility.

———

Any gentleman in a wedding party dresses according to the wishes of the bride and groom.

———

Even though he is not the groom, the best man, like every other gentleman in the wedding party, understands that it is part of his job to look his best. His nails are scrupulously clean, his shoes are well shined, and his hair is freshly cut.

The best man knows that he will be photographed many times during the celebrations surrounding a wedding. He does so with a ready smile, no matter how many times the camera flashes.

Lord of the Ring

The best man knows that one of his most solemn responsibilities on the wedding day is to keep track of the bride's wedding ring. He makes sure he has it in his possession well before he and the groom depart for the ceremony. For safety's sake he may keep it in a small envelope, either in the pocket of his trousers or in the breast pocket of his jacket. Shortly before he and the groom take their places alongside the officiant, he slips the ring onto the little finger of his left hand, keeping his finger crooked at all times.

He understands that the ring carried on the ring bearer's satin cushion is merely for show.

At the appropriate moment in the ceremony, he hands the ring over to the groom or to the officiant. (He will have been given clear instructions at the wedding rehearsal.)

Although he may think it humorous, the best man does not pretend that he has lost the bride's ring just as he and the groom take their places for the ceremony. Such practical jokes have a habit of turning into harsh realities.

GUARD OF HONOR:
THE GROOMSMEN AND USHERS

A gentleman recognizes that an invitation to be a part of a wedding is a compliment, and he responds accordingly. His response, whether he accepts or declines, is gracious, kindly, and grateful.

———

A gentleman does not view an invitation to serve as an usher or a groomsman as "coming in second" to the best man.

———

A groomsman is prepared to perform any task requested of him at the wedding, whether it is lighting a candle, unfurling a white carpet, or escorting the bride's great-grandmother down the aisle, one stately step at a time.

———

If a gentleman is uncertain as to the dress code for any wedding-related celebration or for the rehearsal dinner, he asks the bride or groom for guidance.

Traditional Duties of an Usher or Groomsman

- Accept the invitation to join the wedding party
- Confirm plans as to what he is to wear at the ceremony
- Rent formalwear, or get fitted for a new suit or jacket, as the case requires
- Participate in planning the bachelor party
- Participate in the wedding rehearsal
- Participate in the rehearsal dinner as a guest
- Offer a toast to the bride and groom at the rehearsal dinner, if called upon to do so
- Wake up early, and in good shape, on the morning of the wedding day
- Show up on time for any photo shoots
- Show up on time for the wedding ceremony
- Participate in the wedding reception, mingling with guests and dancing with as many ladies from the bridal party as possible
- Make sure that his rented formalwear, along with all its accessories—including tie, cuff links, and studs—is returned on time

What a Groomsman or Usher
Usually Pays For

- His own travel expenses and lodging related to the wedding ceremony and other wedding-related events—unless the groom or one of the families offers to assist in covering those costs
- Rental of his own formalwear, or, if necessary, the purchase of other appropriate attire
- His own fair share of expenses related to the bachelor party
- His fair share of the cost of a groom's gift from all the groom's attendants
- His own gift for the bride and groom

I'm Wearing This Rented Suit.
But Who Am I?

The terms "groomsman" and "usher" are virtually inter-changeable at most modern weddings. Although the term *groomsman* seems almost to have slipped out of most etiquette guides, it still persists in common wedding parlance, since it is the honorific bestowed on any of the gentlemen asked to stand alongside the groom, in support of him, at his wedding.

Most often, when a groom invites a friend to join his wedding party, he says, "I hope you'll be one of my groomsmen." It's unlikely he would say, "I hope you'll be one of my ushers," which sounds unpleasantly like, "I'm wondering if you'd be one of my pallbearers."

At some ceremonies, however, the two roles are distinct. Even if all the gentlemen in a bridal party are generically known as groomsmen, a few of them may perform a purely ceremonial function—simply joining in the processional. It is the ushers who do the actual work.

This is the case, rare though it may be, when the groom has more attendants than the bride has. As "extra gentlemen" these groomsmen walk up the aisle, side by side, at the start of the processional. The image is rather impressive, actually, since they seem to serve as a sort of de facto guard of honor.

They depart, side by side, at the close of the recessional, following in the train of the ushers, who are coupled with their appointed bridesmaids.

Some wedding parties may even include junior groomsmen, teenage or preteen young gentlemen who are usually relatives of the bride or groom. (Should there be teenage sons from a previous marriage, this is a role they may play, thus giving them a place of recognition on a day when they might well feel forgotten.) They do participate in the wedding rehearsal and are invited to the rehearsal dinner. They are not included on the guest list for the bachelor party, unless it is guaranteed to be a determinedly decorous affair.

Three Things a Gentleman Never Says When Asked to be an Usher or a Groomsman

- "What's up? Wasn't I good enough to be the best man?"
- "What do the bridesmaids look like?"
- "Okay, but only if I can escort one of the Tri Delts."

Friends and Finances

If a gentleman has any experience at all in the world of weddings, he knows that the honor of serving as an attendant comes with a price tag. Not only will he most likely be expected to pay for the rental of his own formalwear (or perhaps even the purchase of a new suit or sports coat and slacks); he will also be expected to purchase a gift for the couple and handle his share of the cost of a gift for the groom, presented to him by all the gentlemen in his wedding party.

If he is an out-of-towner, travel and lodging expenses will also be involved, at least for the days surrounding the wedding. He will probably be invited to a number of parties and receptions in the days and weeks leading up to the ceremony. (Although he may be unable to participate in all these celebrations, he replies to each invitation, promptly, and in the most gentlemanly manner possible.)

If the wedding is taking place in his own town, a gentleman does his best to participate in as many events as he can realistically manage. There is no reason he should feel guilty about saying, "Sorry, I won't be able to make it to the Trim-the-Tree party for Harry and Sally. I've got

Knicks tickets that evening." On the other hand, he might hold off on buying Knicks tickets if he has reason to suspect that a Trim-the-Tree party is in the offing. At the very least, he may consent to arriving a bit late for the Knicks game.

Meanwhile, the traditional bachelor party, with each gentleman paying for his own drinks and dinner, along with a share of the groom's tab for the evening, has now been ramped up so that it often takes the form of a full-blown golf weekend, three days and two nights in Las Vegas, or an all-guy excursion to a tropical resort.

It is a gentleman's prerogative to decide whether his budget and his work schedule will allow him to participate in the full range of festivities associated with a major wedding. Although he does not ask the groom, "What's this going to cost me?" he has every right to make a discreet call to the best man, in hopes of getting a clearer picture of the impending barrage of pre-wedding activities. (The best man handles this phone call with frankness, understanding, diplomacy, and absolute discretion, of course.)

If a gentleman feels that his pockets are not deep enough to permit his participation in the activities surrounding the wedding, he declines the groom's kind invitation, offering a non-money-related explanation. ("I'm really not sure what will be going on at the office in the next few months" might come in handy.)

Should he decide to accept the groom's invitation, knowing that he will be unable to participate fully in the festivities, he keeps his quiet intentions to himself. While he must show up for the wedding proper, make sure he is dressed appropriately, and participate in the necessary gift-giving, he need not commit to a pricey out-of-town bachelor bash. Again, a crowded work schedule makes for a tasteful excuse. (For suggestions for appropriate, affordable wedding gifts, see pages 152–155.)

At the very least, however, a gentleman will treat the bride and groom to dinner and drinks, saying, "Even if I can't make the trip to Barbados, I want to make sure the three of us get to have our own time to celebrate."

A gentleman does not desecrate the bride and groom's vehicle.

———

A gentleman does not break into the groom's honeymoon luggage. He does not do unsightly things to the groom's honeymoon underwear.

———

A gentleman refrains from playing pranks on the groom on the night before the wedding, especially if they might result in unasked-for tattoos, body piercings, or difficult-to-explain bruises.

———

A gentleman knows that "Sorry; I overslept" is never the right excuse, especially if he has left the rest of the wedding party cooling their heels and tapping their feet.

If he has any role in a wedding party, a gentleman knows that nothing, except for a snag in the bride's train, an emergency call from the minister, or a fire alarm in the building, can rightfully delay the start of a wedding ceremony.

————

If he is involved in a wedding in any way—whether he is the groom, a groomsman, the father of the bride, the father of the groom, the ring bearer, or simply a guest—a gentleman always shows up. He also shows up well ahead of time.

————

As a member of the wedding party, a gentleman makes sure he is confident about the agenda for the wedding day (as well as all other festivities in which he may be involved), well ahead of time.

Boys' Night Out

The bachelor party is traditionally seen as the final fling of the groom's single life. As an unchaperoned, male-bonding blowout, it sometimes gets a bad rap. But if the groom and his friends act like the true gentlemen they aspire to be, there is no reason to assume their high jinks will devolve into a full-blown bacchanalia.

The party does not actually require any alcohol. Neither does it require fraternity-style hazing. It can take the form of a casual lunch at a sports bar, a cookout in a friend's backyard, or a well-behaved dinner in the private room of a legendary steak house or a private club. If it is an evening affair, the party may be a dressy one, with the guests wearing black tie; but as a matter of course, the bachelor party is usually a more casual gathering. If the party takes place at a sports bar or around the barbecue grill in a backyard, the guests may even show up in shorts and polo shirts. In any case, fruit juices, sodas, bottled water, and sparkling waters must be offered. (Not everybody drinks alcohol.) There is absolutely no requirement that anyone in the party be poured into a cab or left stumbling his way back to his hotel. Fresh faces, after all, make for fresher photos on the wedding day.

The bachelor party is usually thrown by the groom's friends, with the best man serving as party planner, and the various participants sharing the expense among them, including the expense of entertaining the groom, who will be the evening's guest of honor. The guest list always includes all the groom's attendants, as well as other close friends. Neither the groom's father nor the bride's father is usually part of the evening, except to stop by early in the evening if there is a cocktail hour. If they are invited and wish to join the celebration, their presence will be welcome, nonetheless. Neither of them, however, is expected to pay any part of the bill.

Should the father of the groom be serving as best man, he still leaves it to the younger men of the wedding party to throw the bachelor party. He puts in an appearance, but he does not linger. It is not his job to monitor the behavior for the evening.

Although the temptation is great to stage the bachelor party on the very eve of the wedding, even after the end of the rehearsal dinner, all such temptation should be resisted. If members of the wedding party or other friends are out-of-towners, it is thoughtful to schedule the bachelor party close to the wedding day, perhaps a couple of days before the ceremony. If all the participants in the party live close by, however, there is no reason this celebration should not be scheduled earlier, perhaps on the weekend prior to the wedding.

The groom and his friends may also wish to head out on the town after the rehearsal dinner to top off the evening with some good-natured carousing, but it is their communal, and individual, responsibility to be on time and alert for the next day's ceremony. The groom, in particular, may wish to take a pass on this impromptu activity, since he earnestly intends for his wedding day to be a day he remembers happily—and with a clear head.

The program for the party—if there is any program at all—will be a high-spirited one, with the groom's friends paying good-natured tribute to the groom and recalling happy times they have spent together. The best man serves as master of ceremonies, proposing a toast of his own and inviting the other gentlemen to offer their own jovial expressions of goodwill. A video presentation, including amusing images from the groom's past, is certainly in order. All attempts to embarrass him in an ill-spirited way are completely out of line. So are strippers and unfortunate gag gifts.

The bachelor party also offers an opportunity for the groom's friends, as a group, to present him with their "good-bye" gift. While each of them will be giving a gift to the bride and groom as a couple, the bachelor-party gift is intended for the groom only. It may be as simple or as extravagant as the guests can afford (and the financial means of the guests must be taken into account when the gift is selected). It may be a set of golf clubs or a new pair of golf shoes, a case of good wine, a set of leather-bound books, a set of monogrammed cuff links and studs, a check to help cover part of the honeymoon expenses, or even a collection of airline miles to help cover the travel for the wedding trip.

At the close of the evening, or immediately after he has unwrapped his gift, the groom stands to offer his own toast, thanking his friends for their generosity and for their participation in this magnificent moment in his life.

It is the best man's responsibility to make sure all bills are paid, or that arrangements have been made for paying them, before the evening is done. The groom pays for nothing on this night.

With increasing regularity, the bachelor party now takes the form of an out-of-town trip, perhaps to a resort town, a major city, or some exotic locale. If such are the plans, the budgets of all participants must be kept in mind. It will also be thoughtful to plan a trip that involves at least some activities every member of the party will enjoy. After all, a golf weekend, at a resort focused almost exclusively on the fairway, may not be much fun for an inveterate duffer.

Moreover, when the groom's good friends are planning his bachelor party, they will be wise to remember that cell phone photographs and videos have a way of making their way onto the Internet, where they very likely will be viewed by the bride. Even more disastrous, they may be viewed by her parents. Hence, camera phones should be used judiciously. The activities of the celebration should be planned more judiciously still.

Seven Signs That a Bachelor Party May Be Headed in the Wrong Direction

- There is a distinct possibility somebody might end up spending a night in jail.
- There is an opportunity to tip someone for removing her clothes.
- There will very likely be stories to tell that the groom can't share with his mother.
- There is the potential that the bride will call off the wedding, should she get a full report on the party.
- Drinking and driving might be involved.
- Somebody's passport might be revoked.
- Somebody might come home with a tattoo and not remember where he got it.

Little Big Man: The Ringbearer

Should a wedding party include a ring bearer, his sole function is to be adorable, walk in a straight line, refrain from picking his nose, and resist all temptations to pinch the flower girl. He is the last member of the wedding party to walk down the aisle before the flower girl, who immediately precedes the bride.

He does indeed carry a pair of "wedding rings" on a satin cushion, which he holds in front of him, carefully clasped in both hands. Unless the bride and groom are willing to put major trust in the dependability of a kindergartner, the cushion rings are merely decorative. It is the best man and the maid of honor who carry the actual goods.

The ring bearer wears a mini-tuxedo or a light-colored suit, usually with short pants. The safest option is always for him to join his parents in the congregation once he has successfully made his way down the aisle. A bride who asks a child to stand along with the rest of the wedding party throughout the wedding ceremony is more than likely pushing her luck.

There is a limited window of opportunity for ring bearer service. Unless a three-and-a-half-year-old is extremely precocious (in the right sort of way) and steady on his feet, any tot younger than four merely adds another element of uncertainty to the day. On the other hand, a six-year-old may feel awkward performing a task usually relegated to a post-toddler. The selection must be made carefully, facing the raucous realities of how little boys are prone to behave.

The ring bearer must participate in the wedding rehearsal. It is up to his parents to decide whether the reception is a place where he belongs.

How to Walk a Lady down the Aisle

When a lady of any age, either alone or accompanied by a gentleman, approaches the center aisle at the ceremony, an usher approaches her and asks, "Bride or groom?" If she says, "Bride," he escorts her to a seat on the left side of the congregation, facing the officiant. If she says, "Groom," he escorts her to a seat on the right side. If she says, "Either," he leads her to any available seat midway down the aisle.

In order to escort a lady, he offers his right arm, and she rests her left arm in his elbow. If she is accompanied by a gentleman—her spouse or some other friend—the accompanying gentleman walks behind them.

As they make their way down the aisle, the usher makes some quiet chitchat. ("Frieda and Paolo are a wonderful couple, aren't they?" will usually be enough.) When they have reached a convenient place in the congregation, he pauses and asks, "Will this be all right?" or "How about these seats?" When the lady says yes, the usher steps aside and she steps into the row of seats, followed by her escort. (Should she ask to be seated somewhere else, the usher does his best to accommodate her request.)

If there is more than one lady in the party, each is escorted separately. The usher always takes the older lady first. (This, logically, is a decision the usher must make for himself; he does not ask a lady's age.) If there are enough ushers, even tweens and teenage ladies are escorted down the aisle. (Perhaps a pair of them can share a single usher; he does have two arms, after all.) They will invariably find themselves flattered by the attention. If they are wearing their first pair of heels, they will also be grateful for the assistance.

A Timeline for the Day of Days

The evening before may have been hectic, what with the rehearsal dinner and the celebrations that followed in its tow. Nevertheless, any gentleman involved in the wedding party must keep to a certain regimen once the wedding day is out of the gates.

_____

A Gentleman's Wedding-Day Schedule

This schedule assumes that the wedding ceremony starts at 5:30 P.M.

7:45 A.M.	Wake up.
8 A.M.	Shower. Drink some coffee.
8:30 A.M.	Eat breakfast. Read a newspaper.
9:15 A.M.	Take suit to rental store for alterations. (If the suit fits, this is free time. Use it for a nap. On a wedding day, one can never nap too early or too often.)
10 A.M.	Do something productive—maybe a trip to the gym, a game of golf, or whatever. A movie or a visit to a museum is perfectly acceptable, as long as it gets you home, or back to the hotel, before 1 P.M.
12:30 P.M.	Eat something (unless it's already been included in "golf, or whatever"). Popcorn at the movie multi-plex doesn't count.
1 P.M.	Take a nap.
1:30 P.M.	Start showering and shaving. (Do not wait any later than this.)
2 P.M.	Finish showering and shaving. Put on shirt. Start tying bow tie.

2:45 P.M.	Finish dressing.
3 P.M.	Depart for site of the ceremony or photo shoot.
3:30 P.M.	Arrive at site of ceremony or photo shoot. (If photos will not be taken until after the ceremony, you've gained at least a full hour here.)
4:30 P.M.	Be in place, and alert to duty, for arrival of wedding guests, since a few inevitably arrive inordinately early.
5 P.M.	Guests start arriving, in earnest.
5:30 P.M.	Processional begins.
6 P.M.	Ceremony concludes.
6:30 P.M.	Line up for wedding photos, or depart for reception.
6:50 P.M.	Arrive at wedding reception, unless photo shoot is still under way.
7:15–10 P.M.	Enjoy reception; dance with brides-maids and others; eat something.
10 P.M.	Have a nightcap, if desirable and advisable.

III.

PATERNAL GUIDANCE

The Father of the Bride,
The Father of the Groom

COMMANDER-IN-CHIEF:
THE FATHER OF THE BRIDE

The father of the bride rejoices in
the prospect of his daughter's
impending nuptials.

———

If he does not rejoice immediately
at the prospect of the impending
nuptials, the father of the bride seizes
an early opportunity to offer his
sage counsel and advice.

———

A wise father of the bride
understands that "counsel and
advice" are not the same things as
"caution and warnings."

———

The father of the bride does his best to
like his future son-in-law.

If the father of the bride is not well
acquainted with the groom-to-be,
he gets to know him as well as he can,
as soon as possible.

————

The father of the bride knows that a
simple e-mail exchange is no way to get
to know and appreciate the man who is
marrying his daughter. A lengthy lunch,
just between the two of them, is a
much better way to start.

————

At his first lunch date with his prospective
son-in-law, the father of the bride picks up
the tab, understanding that, in most cases,
it is merely the first of many bills he will
be paying over the coming months.

————

The father of the bride understands that,
traditionally, he and the bride's mother are
responsible for all expenses related to the
wedding ceremony and reception.

The father of the bride understands, or is relieved to learn, that age-old traditions related to who pays for what in the marriage game may now be outmoded.

———

If necessary and appropriate, the father of the bride and the bride's mother, along with any participating stepparents, sit down with the bride and groom for a frank discussion of the wedding budget, clearly delineating lines of financial responsibility: Who will be paying for the bride's dress? (She may well be intent on paying for it herself, in order to get the "mother of the bride" issue out of the picture.) Who will be paying for the church service, including all fees attendant upon the rental of the church, historic site, synagogue, hotel ballroom, or other venue?

Nowadays, this discussion must be open, frank, and clear, so that participants (the bride and bridegroom included) understand precisely what their job responsibilities are.

————

The father of the bride understands that the best way to share the wedding expenses is to delegate certain expenditures to various participating parties.

————

If the father of the bride has a premonition that the cost of the wedding may be getting out of hand, he discusses the matter calmly and directly with his daughter and with the mother of the bride.

————

The father of the bride accepts the fact that, nowadays, when others may be footing a portion of the bill, he may not have sole control over the purse strings. Nevertheless, he stays in the loop as the wedding plans proceed.

The father of the bride never uses
money as a weapon.

————

The father of the bride does not
grouse about the costs of the wedding.
Neither does he brag about how much
he is spending. He knows, in fact,
that grousing, in many cases,
is its own ill-mannered form
of bragging.

————

A gentleman knows that the depth
of his pockets does not demonstrate
the depth of his love.

————

Unless he has serious concerns
about the wedding plans, for reasons
related to morality, finances, faith,
or simple good taste, his only
comment is, "Jessica, dear, I just want
this day to be everything you ever
dreamed it would be."

Traditional Duties of the Father of the Bride

- Give his consent to the impending marriage
- Treat his prospective son-in-law to lunch
- Invite the groom's parents for a private dinner or lunch, with the bride and groom not included
- Listen as attentively as possible as his wife and daughter describe the ceremony they envision
- Discuss the wedding budget with the bride-to-be and her mother
- Do his best to make sure communication is clear, in terms of finances and other plans, especially if stepfathers and stepmothers are involved
- Participate in planning the guest list
- Stick to the budget, at least the part of it that concerns him
- Talk to his banker, if necessary
- Get fitted for his formalwear well ahead of time
- Get his hair cut two days before the wedding
- Make a toast at the rehearsal dinner
- Show up on time for the ceremony
- Escort the bride down the aisle, either on his own or along with the bride's mother
- Serve as host, moving about the room, at the wedding reception
- Pay the bills up through the ceremony and reception, but no farther

What the Father of the Bride Traditionally Pays For

- All costs of the wedding ceremony and reception, including rental of the church or ballroom, the bride's dress, bouquets for her attendants, fees for musicians, caterers, the wedding planner

Or:
- His portion of the cost of the ceremony and reception, if the bride and groom are picking up part of the tab, or if stepparents are sharing the cost
- Dinner, lunch, or drinks with the groom's parents, especially if they are not well acquainted
- All costs for an engagement dinner, if one has been planned
- Rental of formalwear for the groom's attendants—unless they are expected to pay for their own rentals, or the rentals are being covered by the groom's parents.
- Rental of his own formalwear
- A gift for the newlyweds, from him and his spouse

Rent a Church?
But Didn't I Already Write a Pledge Check?

More often than not, a wedding fee will be charged for the use of a house of worship, even if the bride and groom are members of the congregation. The father of the bride will be wise to check ahead of time to determine precisely what expenses are covered by that fee. (Does it include an honorarium for the musicians? What about the sextons or other staff? Is the minister usually paid for conducting the service?) Most congregations have a wedding coordinator on staff, or a committee of volunteers who can answer such questions. And such questions should be asked, as unashamedly and as soon as possible.

Should he be asked for his daughter's hand in marriage, unless he has serious doubts about the character of the groom-to-be, the father of the bride-to-be says yes.

————

If the bride- and groom-to-be are living on their own, the father of the bride understands that, in most cases, his consent is being requested merely as a gesture of respect and love.

A gentleman does not bad-mouth his future son-in-law in public. If he must vent, he does so in the presence of his spouse, his minister, or his therapist.

————

If he does not approve of the groom-to-be, the father of the bride expresses his concerns to the bride, calmly and quietly, in a private conversation involving just the two of them.

The father of the bride understands that, ultimately, his daughter's choice of a mate is her own decision.

———

The father of the bride never says, "I hope I never have to say, 'I told you so.'"

———

A gentleman never says, "I told you so."

The father of the bride remembers that the wedding in the works is not *his* wedding. Neither is it the wedding of the mother of the bride.

Three Things Any Prospective Son-in-Law Would Be Glad to Hear From His Future Father-in-Law:

- "I'm proud to call you a member of our family."
- "Sam, I don't think Jennifer could have made a finer choice."
- "It thrills me to see how much you and Jenny love each other."

Three Things No Potential Son-in-Law Should Hear From His Future Father-in-Law:

- "You better treat her right, son. I've always got a .22 in my gun rack."
- "I hope you can afford her."
- "Personally, I think she can do better; but I guess you're what she wants."

Walking the Walk

During the wedding proper, the father of the bride's only ceremonial duty is to escort his daughter down the aisle. Simple though this task may seem, it is part of the bride's most exciting moment of the day—the moment when her friends and family first see her in the dress she has dreamed of all her life, smiling her brightest and looking her most radiant. It is likely to be a highly emotional moment, so the father of the bride should take a deep breath before taking the first step down the white carpet.

The bride walks on his right side, her left arm resting in his right elbow. Once they are standing in front of the officiant, he waits until he is asked to "give" her to her new husband; then, after giving her a gentle buss on the cheek, he steps aside and joins his spouse, who will be sitting in the congregation.

In some traditions, however, both of the bride's parents accompany her down the aisle and remain on the dais throughout the ceremony. What's more, in today's world of blended families, the bride may ask that her stepfather, or her father *and* her stepfather, walk her down the aisle. In every case, the father of the bride bows to his daughter's wishes.

Some brides, of course, may not wish to be "given away" by anyone. Thus, rather than asking, "Who gives this woman to be married?" the officiant may ask, "Who presents this woman to be married?" The father's traditional response, "Her mother and I" (or "I do," if the father is alone) remains appropriate. Or there may be no "giving away" or "presenting" at all, in which case the father of the bride simply kisses his daughter lightly on the cheek and then takes his place in the congregation.

More often than not, a wedding planner, or a wedding coordinator provided by the church or synagogue, will be on hand to make sure the bride and her father begin their progress down the aisle at precisely the appropriate moment.

Double Dads

In situations where the bride is particularly close to her stepfather, she may ask that he assume much of the role usually played by the father of the bride. If she has largely been brought up in his household or if he is covering the lion's share of the wedding expenses, this decision should come as no surprise to the father of the bride. As in virtually every other aspect of the wedding, the father of the bride accedes to her wishes.

At some point close to the wedding day— the rehearsal dinner will probably offer an appropriate moment—the father of the bride makes sure to tell the parents of his future son-in-law what a fine job they have done in raising their son.

———

The father of the bride makes sure to carry a pocket handkerchief, since he knows he may very well need it to wipe away his tears of joy.

The Receiving Line

Other than the groom himself, the father of the bride is traditionally the only gentleman with a place in the receiving line at a wedding reception.

Here is the traditional line up for those greeting or "receiving" the guests:

- Mother of the bride (if she is serving as hostess, even in an honorary capacity)
- Mother of the groom
- Father of the bride
- Bridesmaids
- Bride
- Groom

Often, however, the father of the bride does not participate in the receiving line at all. Instead, as the host of the party, he may choose to work the room, making sure all the guests are well served and all details are being attended to. This arrangement is particularly convenient when both a father and a stepfather of the bride are on hand, since it saves the bride from having to decide who takes precedence. (Making such a choice can be a real challenge if the bride is equally devoted to the two of them, or if her stepfather is picking up a sizable portion of the tab for the party.)

If the bride's father has remarried, his decision not to join the receiving line also forestalls some of the potential awkwardness the bride's stepmother may feel.

If the bride and groom are throwing their own reception, and nobody's parents have had any substantial involvement in the planning or financing of the event, they may, of course, take pride of place, standing at the head of the line as the first to greet their guests and accept their friends' good wishes.

The father of the groom, the best man, and the groomsmen are not part of the receiving line. Instead, their responsibility is to be congenial and make sure as many ladies as possible, no matter what their ages, have had a chance for a dance.

Dancing Class
THE FIRST DANCE FOR THE REST OF YOUR LIFE

Although the dancing at the reception may have begun long before the arrival of the wedding party, the groom is always the first to dance with the bride.

Their first dance is usually announced by either the best man, a member of the band, or the deejay. Traditionally, the announcer says, "And now, ladies and gentlemen, let me introduce to you Mr. and Mrs. Lloyd Peter Gosdale III!" But he might just as easily say, should the couple prefer it, "And now, please join me in welcoming our first lady and first gentleman of the evening—Lindsay Hasthaus and Pete Gosdale!"

Everyone else leaves the floor for the couple's first dance.

Once the bride and groom have danced, others may begin to return to the dance floor. Usually, however, they wait until a few couples-of-honor have begun at least one ceremonial, albeit perfunctory, swirl around the room.

After the bride and groom have danced their first dance . . .

• The bride dances with her father while

the groom dances with his mother, and the bride's mother dances with the groom's father.

- As the guests return to the dance floor, the bride's parents dance together, as do the groom's parents. (Should they be divorced and remarried, they dance with their respective spouses.) Since the bride and groom will be dancing together as well, the moment becomes a celebration of two generations.
- During the course of the reception, the groom dances as often as possible with the bride, although he graciously allows the best man, the groomsmen, and the brothers and uncles of the bride to cut in, provided they ask politely.
- While others are dancing with the bride, the groom dances with his grandmother, the bride's grandmother, and other ladies of a certain age.

If the father of the bride is not an accomplished dancer, he invests in a few dancing lessons in the weeks leading up to the ceremony.

GENTLEMANLY GENES:
THE FATHER OF THE GROOM

The father of the groom tries his best to establish pleasant social relations with the bride's parents. He realizes, however, that they are on tap to become his son's in-laws, not his own.

————

As the host of the rehearsal dinner, the father of the groom helps plan a celebration that is in line with the general tone of the wedding weekend. He does not attempt to outdo the father of the bride in terms of spending.

————

The father of the groom hosts a rehearsal dinner that is within his means, and in line with the wishes of the bride and groom. If a backyard cookout is what they want, a backyard cookout is what he provides.

If he and the mother of the groom are asked to help cover the costs of the wedding, the father of the groom does so, to the best of his abilities.

———————

The father of the groom may wish to contribute toward the costs of the honeymoon. If he does so, however, he makes sure that agreement remains a private matter between him and his son. It is up to the groom to decide when such information should be shared with the bride.

———————

If the father of the groom and his wife are out-of-towners, they do their best to introduce themselves to people with whom they are not acquainted.

———————

The father of the groom may not be the official host of the wedding ceremony, but he need not be the forgotten man of the wedding weekend.

The father of the groom does his best
to console his wife, should she be less
than happy with the number of guests
apportioned to her for the ceremony
and reception.

———

The father of the groom, relieved of most
of the responsibilities and expenses
related to the wedding, remains at his
most congenial throughout the entire
planning process—especially on
the wedding day.

TRADITIONAL DUTIES OF THE FATHER OF THE GROOM

- Make a call to the father of the bride, or invite him out for lunch, drinks, or a golf game as soon as the wedding is a sure thing
- Make sure, to the best of his ability, that communication is clear among all members of the groom's family, especially if stepparents are involved
- Counsel the mother of the groom as the guest list is developed
- Offer a brief, appropriate toast at the rehearsal dinner
- Get fitted for his formalwear well ahead of time
- Get his hair cut two days before the wedding
- Show up on time for the ceremony, and for any photo shoots
- Serve as his son's best man, if requested to do so
- Accompany his wife down the aisle, if he is not a member of the wedding party
- Participate, as a pleasant, good-natured guest, in the wedding reception

Although the father of the groom is often asked to serve as his son's best man, this is not a longstanding tradition. It is up to the groom to select his own attendants, usually from his own generation.

————

The groom's family may offer to pay for rental of formalwear for the groom's attendants, but this is by no means a necessity. If they are making this gesture, however, they make sure the groom's attendants are aware of it early in the game.

What the Father of the Groom Traditionally Pays For

- All costs of the rehearsal dinner, including food, flowers, music, and any other entertainment—or his share of the costs, if stepparents are helping cover the expenses
- A gift for the bride and groom (cash, if it seems appropriate)
- Rental of his own formalwear
- Transportation and lodging for himself and his spouse, should they be out-of-towners

Glass Ceilings

The rehearsal dinner is a high-spirited occasion, the perfect time for the exchange of toasts. (The only obligatory toast at the wedding reception is one from the best man, offered as the first "official" introduction of the married couple to their family and friends.)

The first toasts of the evening are offered once all the guests are seated and have been served. (They do not begin, of course, until after any blessing has been offered or grace has been said.)

The First Round of Toasts is Brief:

- A toast from the father of the groom, welcoming the guests
- A toast from the father of the bride, responding to the welcome

A Toast by the Father of the Groom
at the Rehearsal Dinner

Mary Anne and I are so grateful to all of you
for joining us this evening. Obviously, we've
known Ted for a number of years, but we
already feel that we've known and loved
Gloria forever.

Here's to a beautiful evening, a beautiful
tomorrow, and beautiful years to come.

Hear! Hear!

A Toast by the Father of the Bride
at the Rehearsal Dinner

Gerry and Mary Anne, this is a beautiful
evening, filled with friends and family. Thank
you for bringing it together. And thank you
for Ted. Gloria deserves no less, and she
could find no one finer.

So here's to you, to all of us here, and
most especially, to the bride and groom.

Hear! Hear!

Once the dessert course has been served, other toasts may follow. The best man serves as emcee for that portion of the evening, doing his best to make sure the toasts proceed according to a preestablished agenda and—as best as possible—according to a set time schedule.

A REASONABLE LINEUP OF TOASTERS MIGHT INCLUDE:

- a toast from the best man
- a toast from a groomsman, representing the groom's attendants
- a toast from a bridesmaid, representing the bride's attendants
- a toast from a sibling of the bride
- a toast from a sibling of the groom
- a closing toast, jointly delivered, from the bride and groom

A Toast by the Best Man at the Rehearsal Dinner

Mr. and Mrs. Lawrence asked me to serve as emcee this evening, and they asked me to keep it short. So, I want to say, as simply as possible: Ted, you've been my best friend since our freshman year at Albermore; you have always done great things for me. Tomorrow, I'll be doing an even greater thing for you, since I'll be the one who gives you the ring that you give to Gloria.

So now I say, "Here's to the bride and groom. Hear! Hear!"

A groomsman knows his toast may be headed the wrong way if . . .

- it mentions the groom's past girlfriends, or, even worse, a previous spouse.
- it includes a story that gives the bride's family second thoughts about their future son-in-law-to-be.
- it comes after more than a couple of cocktails, or after 11 o'clock in the evening.
- it lasts longer than 90 seconds.

A Toast by a Groomsman at the Rehearsal Dinner

Let me start by saying thank you to Mr. and Mrs. Lawrence for a great party. Meanwhile, Frieda and Paolo, I know I speak for all the other guys in the wedding when I say how honored we are to be part of tomorrow, and to be part of your lives. You, Frieda, are as beautiful as any bride could be; and you, Paolo, look pretty nervous.

Tomorrow, we all promise to show up on time, wear the right shoes, and stand up tall. You've made us proud. We intend to do the same for you.

We love you. You have our every best wish in the world. Hear! Hear!

A Toast by the Groom at the Rehearsal Dinner

Mom and Dad [or "Dad and Teresa," or "Mom and Malcolm"], thank you for this wonderful evening. You are the best ever.

Both Gloria and I thank you and say, "Here's to us"; "Here's to you"; "Here's to a life filled with love for all of us."

Hear! Hear!

A gentleman knows that it is absolutely proper to toast the wedding couple with a nonalcoholic beverage. An empty glass is the only unacceptable option.

————

While a great many of the guests at the wedding reception may be his personal friends, the father of the groom realizes he is not the host of the evening. He does not take credit for a party he did not give.

If the father of the groom is not fully pleased with anything about the wedding or the reception, he keeps his opinions to himself.

————

At the close of the evening, he makes sure to express his gratitude to the mother and father of the bride. "Thank you, Hannah and Joel," he says. "I think we've got a very happy couple on our hands."

A Note from the Father of the Groom to His Potential Daughter-in-Law

A particularly thoughtful father of the groom may wish to send a handwritten note to his prospective daughter-in-law, scheduled to arrive a couple of days before the wedding. It might read:

Dear Gloria,

Beverly and I feel truly blessed to have you in our lives. Our own eyes light up every time we see the light in Ted's eyes, each time he looks at you.

You have brought a new sense of joy into Ted's life, and we rejoice in the beauty you share, not just with him, but with us as well.

Thank you for being part of our family. Please know that you are a gift to us all.

All my love,
Gerry

NB: The father of the groom makes absolutely no mention about his or his wife's hopes for future grandchildren. Such jumping the gun, overpressurizing the newlyweds, and rushing ahead of the game are in extremely poor taste, no matter how well-intentioned.

A gentleman knows that it is never too early to say kind and welcoming words. He also knows they can never be said too often. He is confident that he will never have to take them back.

IV.

THE HONOUR OF YOUR PRESENCE IS REQUESTED

A Gentleman Guest at a Wedding

The Fortunate Few

When a gentleman is invited to a
wedding, he takes the invitation as a
sincere compliment, offered by friends
who have chosen to include
him in one of life's most
joyous celebrations.

———

A gentleman responds to a
wedding invitation as quickly as
possible, letting the host and/or hostess
know whether he will or will not be
able to attend.

———

A gentleman understands that "as quickly
as possible" means within a week—or
even sooner, since he knows that caterers
are probably being engaged.

If no reply card is enclosed with the invitation, a gentleman mails his reply to the return address shown on the invitation envelope.

––––––––

If, for reasons of haste or extreme informality, a gentleman receives a wedding invitation by phone, e-mail, or some other social networking system, he may feel free to respond in kind.

––––––––

A gentleman knows, however, that a written note always trumps a phone message, an e-mail, or any other sort of electronic communication. A handwritten note, he knows, is never overkill.

When accepting a wedding invitation, even from the closest of friends—a gentleman is always right to use the simplest, most traditional third-person response, handwritten in ink, on a white or ecru card:

> Mr. Flavius Hallnook
> accepts with pleasure
> Mrs. Bridesaplenty's
> [or "Mr. and Mrs. Parsewell's" or "Ms. Titus
> and Mr. Thomas's"] kind invitation
> for Saturday evening, May 27th.

When declining a wedding invitation, a gentleman is always correct to stick with the most traditional format:

> Mr. Flavius Hallnook
> regrets that he is unable to accept
> Mrs. Bridesaplenty's kind invitation
> for May 27th due to a previous engagement
> [or "due to travel plans" or, in the worst
> possible situation, "due to a death in his family"].

A gentleman knows that writing in the simple third-person is always the best option, especially when declining an invitation, since it requires no extended explanation for not attending the ceremony. Nevertheless, he makes sure to extend his best wishes to the couple at his very earliest opportunity.

Traditional Duties of a Gentleman Invited to a Wedding

- Respond to the invitation as soon as possible
- Send or deliver a gift to the return address on the invitation envelope, *before* the day of the wedding
- Participate in showers and other celebrations, as his schedule and budget allow
- Get a fresh haircut and have his shoes shined in anticipation of the wedding day
- Offer a toast at the rehearsal dinner, should he be included in that celebration
- Refrain from offering toasts at any celebration related to the wedding, unless he has been specifically invited to do so
- Show up on time for the ceremony (especially if he has been invited to sit "within the ribbons") (See page 146.)
- Behave himself during the ceremony, which means no fidgeting, no chatting back and forth with other members of the congregation, and absolutely no use of electronic devices
- Stand and turn to face the rear of the church, the garden, or the hotel ballroom, as the bride makes her way down the aisle. As she moves toward the altar, he turns forward as she passes him.
- Turn off all electronic devices, including camera phones, during the ceremony
- Subject himself to the receiving line at the

reception, no matter how long it may be, introducing himself to any member of the wedding party to whom his name may not be familiar, taking special care to introduce any guest he may have brought along

- Dance as much, and as well, as he can
- Depart as soon as he wishes, once he has greeted the wedding party and behaved in a sociable way for an acceptable period of time. (Forty-five minutes is an acceptable period of time.)

What a Wedding Guest Usually Pays For

- A gift for the bride and groom
- His own transportation and lodging, if the wedding is out of town
- Rental of his own formalwear, if required
- His own transportation and lodging for the bachelor party, should he be invited and if it takes place out of town

A gentleman arrives for the wedding ceremony at least 20 minutes before its scheduled starting time.

————

Should a gentleman arrive after the wedding ceremony has begun, he stands at the rear of the congregation until the service has concluded. He never walks down the aisle once the ceremony is under way. He makes sure to step out of the way during the recessional.

————

If a gentleman attends a wedding ceremony that is a religious service, he respects the traditions of that religion. He need not cross himself or kneel unless he feels moved to do so, but he does, at the very least, stand and sit along with the rest of the congregation.

————

If a gentleman arrives at a wedding ceremony and is offered a yarmulke, he puts it on.

A gentleman does not bring a date or other guest to a wedding unless his invitation specifically suggests that he do so, either by mentioning the name of his significant other or by adding "and guest" directly after his name.

————

If a gentleman's significant other has been omitted from a wedding invitation, he may feel free to ask if that person may join him in the evening's celebration. He makes that request as soon as possible after receiving his invitation.

————

A gentleman does not usually consider a person he has known for less than a week to be a "significant other."

If a gentleman is told he may not
bring a guest to the wedding, he does
not take umbrage. He may elect to
attend the ceremony and skip the
reception, put in only a brief appearance
at the reception, or simply send
along his simplest, most
tasteful regrets.

————

Unless he is the designated
photographer for the wedding
ceremony, a gentleman does not bring
along his own camera.

————

Upon arriving for the ceremony, a
gentleman follows the directions
of the ushers.

If an usher asks him, "Bride or groom?" it is up to the gentleman to decide, based on his friendship with the couple, whether he wishes to sit on the "bride's side" (the left side of the congregation, facing the wedding party) or the "groom's side" (the right side of the congregation, facing the wedding party). If it makes no difference to him, he says, "Either."

———

Unless an usher offers to lead him down the aisle, a single gentleman usually finds his own place in a convenient, easily accessible seat, alongside friends of his own, if he is lucky.

Within Limits

On rare occasions, enclosed with a wedding invitation, a gentleman may find a small card indicating that he is to be seated "within the ribbons." This card assures him a seat close to the chancel or the chuppah—if he arrives on time. It may even indicate the pew, or row, in which he is to be seated.

Even if the ceremony is a simple one, and even if the gathering is small, a gentleman finds it an honor to be asked to sit "within the ribbons."

If a guest has neglected this special privilege and shows up five minutes before the start of the ceremony, he has no reason to presume any preferential treatment, no matter what card he presents to the usher.

If a gentleman is in the company of a lady, he allows an usher to offer his arm and walk with her down the aisle, the gentleman following them. He knows that it is up to the lady, with the advice of the usher, to select the row or pew in which she wishes to sit. Once she has stepped into that row, the gentleman follows her, and the two of them take their seats.

————

At the conclusion of the ceremony, and once all the members of the wedding party—including the mothers of the bride and groom—have departed, a gentleman steps into the aisle, allowing the lady to then step in front of him. He then walks behind her or alongside her as they make their way down the aisle.

A gentleman does not snap cell-phone photos during a wedding ceremony. Knowing that a cell phone may very well ruin the line of his suit pants, and knowing that he will not be needing it during the ceremony, he will wisely elect to leave it in his car.

———

A gentleman does not send text messages during a wedding ceremony. Neither does he check his incoming messages. A gentleman turns off his cell phone and all other electronic devices during the ceremony.

———

If a gentleman must make or receive a phone call during the wedding reception, he steps into a hallway, onto a porch, or—at the very least—away from the center of the celebration. Otherwise, he is likely to find himself shouting, in hopes of being heard above the hullaballoo.

Wishing Well

Long-held tradition decreed that, upon learning of a couple's engagement, a gentleman might say, "Congratulations" to the groom-to-be, but only offer his "best wishes" to the bride-in-line. The reasoning was that extending "congratulations" to the bride implied that she had, in some way, "snagged" a husband after waiting to "catch him," lest she live out her life as a maiden aunt, old maid, or Nobel-winning physicist. (Poor thing.)

"Congratulations" is now accepted as the right thing to say to either party, or to the couple. "Best wishes," for good or ill, tends to smack of something one might tack on at the close of a business letter or, even worse, something one might say in the receiving line at a funeral.

A gentleman dresses appropriately
for the wedding ceremony, whatever
time of day it is held.

If a gentleman is uncertain as to the
dress code for a wedding celebration,
he makes a phone call or sends an e-mail,
asking straightforwardly what he
should wear.

Dressing for Weddings . . .

The wedding begins at	The invitation was
11 A.M.	engraved or thermographed
1 P.M.	photocopied
4 P.M.	e-mailed
5 P.M.	handmade by the bride
5:30 P.M.	printed
7 P.M.	obviously engraved

Anywhere, Any Place

The Reception Will Be Held In	A Gentleman Wears
a university or alumni club	suit and tie
the VFW hall	sports coat and tie
the groom's favorite sports bar	sports coat and tie
a cow pasture	sandals
the church social hall	sports coat or suit
a major country club or hotel ballroom	black tie

The Gift of Giving

A gentleman does not view the giving of wedding gifts precisely as an obligation. He does his best not to feel that the mere unsealing of a wedding invitation puts him under any sort of duress.

On the other hand, he knows that, once he has accepted an invitation to a wedding, a round of gift shopping—either on foot or online—is almost inevitably in the offing.

The truth of the matter is that, according to the most arcane rules of formal etiquette, unless a gentleman accepts the invitation and actually attends the wedding reception, he is under no obligation to send a gift. The theory behind this bit of hairsplitting is that the wedding itself is a civil ceremony and a public event, which anybody has the right to witness. The officiant, after all, *does* say, "By the powers vested in me by the State of Iowa [or wherever], I now pronounce you . . ."

The reception, then, is a private party following the public sealing of a legal contract. The reception guests, having been chosen from among the great teeming masses, might logically wish to demonstrate their gratitude with a tribute to the newlyweds.

A gentleman never *has* to give a gift to anybody, of course. If such were the case, what he gave would not actually be a gift. Nevertheless, he knows that the expectation is that, once a wedding invitation has been accepted, a gift will be forthcoming.

Even if he's never bought anything for anybody, ever before in his life, a gentleman will discover that the task of purchasing and sending a wedding gift is considerably less than daunting.

In today's world, a great many prenuptial couples visit a number of stores and websites, and create a "registry" of gifts they would like to receive. These lists may include traditional gifts such as china, crystal, and silver (which skew toward the costly); but couples are now registering online and at well-known department stores for everyday-useful items, such as small appliances, linens, easy-to-wash dishes, and glassware.

A gentleman knows that gift-giving is not a competition. The perfect gift is the one that the starting-out couple precisely wants and needs.

If a gentleman wants to know if and where a couple is registered, he simply asks them. (It continues to be poor taste for a couple to distribute, far and wide, a list that brings the world at large up-to-date with,

"In case you were wondering . . . here's where we're registered.")

A gentleman does not disparage online shopping, if it makes his life easier—and especially if it allows him to select a gift within his price range, that the couple actually can use.

In cases when the couple has elected not to register for gifts (this is often the case when one, or both, of the partners has been married before, or when they have already set up housekeeping), a gentleman uses his imagination to select the best possible gift for the couple. If they are personal friends of his, he can be confident with a bottle of their favorite wine, or with a gift card for a local restaurant where he knows they like to celebrate. He might also treat them to hard-to-get tickets to an upcoming concert or a major sports event—but only if he is fully confident that they are both fans of the concert's headliner, or that they both root for the same team.

If a couple has been living under the same roof for any length of time, an elaborate wedding gift is unnecessary. Unless a gentleman knows for sure that the couple wants china and crystal goblets to complete their place settings, or that they truly can use a new chip-and-dip set, he steers away from "newlywed" gifts of any sort.

He always feels confident in offering a bottle of champagne (with a couple of champagne flutes attached, perhaps); tickets to an upcoming symphony concert or hockey game; a gift card at a restaurant that the couple enjoys; greens fees at a local golf course; or a hefty handful of coupons for movie tickets. What's more, he knows that a contribution to a charitable cause, given in the couple's honor, is always in perfect taste.

A gentleman also knows that a simple, elegant picture frame, to display a photograph from the honeymoon, is always the unquestionably perfect gift—no matter how many times either party has been married before. If it is a gift for a first wedding, it is even more perfect the second time around. It is not only right for pictures of weddings and honeymoons; it is also just the right frame for first baby pictures and grandbaby pictures as well.

Widely Scattered Showers

If a gentleman is a close friend of the couple, he may receive invitations to a number of parties anticipating the upcoming wedding. Unless the party is clearly billed as a "shower" or some other occasion at which gifts are expected (such as a "Stock the Bar" or "Trim the Tree" party), he is under no obligation to bring along a present.

At any rate, a shower does not demand an extravagant gift, especially if a gentleman also intends to send a wedding gift. Such is definitely the case when it comes to showers staged by coworkers for a fellow employee. In such situations—if he has already picked out his wedding present, and especially if he will also be attending one or more other events at which gifts will be expected, he may choose to bring no gift at all. No explanations or excuses are required.

A gentleman does not bring a gift to an engagement party (unless the gift is absolutely generic, such as a bottle of wine). What's more, he does not bring his wedding gift to a shower.

As a general rule, a gentleman does not give cash as a wedding or shower gift, unless it is specifically requested. Some showers, for example, take the form of a "money tree" party, at which guests are asked to pitch in toward a major gift, such as a sound system, or a specific project, such as adding a deck to the couple's bungalow.

At some wedding receptions, however, a gentleman will discover a container, perhaps a bowl or a bag, set out unmistakably for monetary gifts. If a gentleman has already sent a substantial gift to the couple, he may choose to make another modest contribution to their happy future. Or he may choose to write a check.

Otherwise Engaged
Untraditional Ceremonies, Everywhere

From time to time, a gentleman may find himself invited to a wedding ceremony that—at least by his standards—is unconventional, untraditional, or even unusual. That ceremony may celebrate the legal union of a couple who have lived together for years; the marriage of a couple, one or both of whom have been married multiple times before; the marriage of a much older man to a younger woman; the marriage of a considerably older woman to a considerably younger man; the marriage of two people of different faiths, races, or ethnic traditions; or the marriage of a couple who met via the Internet. In such cases, a gentleman may have second thoughts about whether he wishes to attend the ceremony, or even acknowledge the invitation. He has every right to decline the invitation, of course, but it would be less than gentlemanly of him to ignore it.

Even if he does not approve of the upcoming nuptials, a gentleman always considers it an honor to be included on the invitation list. If he plans to attend the ceremony, he responds promptly, so he can be included in the head count. If he does not plan to participate, he makes that decision known, as soon as possible.

A gentleman does not moralize about his decision—neither to the soon-to-be married couple, nor to any of their mutual acquaintances. Instead, he sends the simplest, most direct response. (See page 138.) Under no circumstances does he fire off a high-handed note saying, "I regret to inform you that I will not be at your wedding. I'm sorry you've chosen to take this unfortunate step." If such are his feelings, it would be hypocritical of him, of course, to send a gift.

Predictably enough, extraordinary ceremonies are often staged in extraordinary places—on a hillside overlooking the ocean, in a backwoods cabin, in a bowling alley, or in the corner bar where the couple first met. The invitation may leave a gentleman in a quandary as to what to wear, how to behave, or whether he should send a gift. If a gentleman has any uncertainties as to what he should wear or how he may be asked to participate in the celebration, he simply contacts one of the prospective spouses, asks his questions, and quiets his concerns.

A gentleman does not bring his gift along
with him to the wedding ceremony.
Instead, he has it delivered, or delivers it
himself, a few days before—or even a
few days after—the wedding.

———

If, for some reason, a gentleman
finds he must bring his gift along with
him to the wedding reception (not the
ceremony), he places it on the "gift table,"
which will usually be located close
to the door. He does not attempt to present
it directly to the bride, whose hands will
already be busy with her bouquet.

———

A gentleman always encloses a
card with his gift.

If a gentleman has received no acknowledgment of his gift after a period of several weeks—and especially if he has not delivered the gift by hand—he has every right to make a call, saying, "I was just checking to make sure Bromwell's delivered your gift. I wanted to make sure it got there in time for the wedding."

———

If a gentleman never receives an acknowledgment of his gift—much less a thank-you note—he assumes either that the note has been lost in the mail, or that the bride and groom have lost their collective sense of propriety.

———

A gentleman knows that he has six months to get his wedding gift to a newlywed couple. After that period of time, he lets the matter drop.

No matter how late he may be in
delivering a wedding gift, a gentleman
does not apologize for his tardiness.
Instead, he says, "I hope you know that I
can still hear those wedding bells."

———

If the couple has requested "no gifts,"
a gentleman respects their wishes.
He may, however, wish to treat them to
drinks or dinner, sometime shortly after
the ceremony. (He does not attempt
to crowd this well-meaning gesture
into the already jam-packed
pre-wedding schedule.)

Tripping off the Tongue

If a gentleman is less than enthusiastic upon hearing about an upcoming union, he will be wise to think twice (or even more times) before he makes any comment. If he thinks long and hard enough, he will probably make no comment at all.

When either one or both of the prospective spouses have been married previously, he does not say . . .

- "Think this one will stick?"
- "Fifth time's the charm, huh?"
- "She's not wearing white, is she?"
- "I can't believe you're going to have this wedding in a church."
- "Are you sure that first marriage of his was really annulled?"

When one member of the couple is significantly older than the other, he does not say . . .

- "Well, here's to you, Mrs. Robinson."
- "Are you older than her dad?"
- "I guess children are out of the question."
- "You think she's going to be this happy when you're 75 and she's 40?"
- "What does Marcie think about having a stepmother who's younger than she is?"

Instead, he keeps his quick quips, objections, and probing questions to himself. After all, a gentleman never intentionally hurts another person's feelings.

A gentleman always rejoices in the union of two happy people, as best he can. If he does not rejoice, he keeps his discontentment to himself.

———

A gentleman does not crash weddings. Neither does he crash wedding receptions.

———

At a wedding reception, a gentleman makes sure his comments are always in scrupulously good taste, especially when he is making conversation with people to whom he has just been introduced. He may think he is being clever with a flippant remark such as "I've got to hand it to Maria for getting Maurice to the altar. That's something his 250 other girlfriends could never do"— until he realizes that he is talking to Maria's grandfather.

If a gentleman is asked to pose for photographs at the wedding reception or other wedding celebrations—whether the photos are being taken for the local newspaper or for the bride's own scrapbook—he participates happily.

————

In the receiving line at a wedding reception, a gentleman always introduces himself to any member of the wedding party with whom he is not well acquainted. He makes sure to pronounce his name clearly.

————

If a gentleman is in the company of a lady, she precedes him in the receiving line. Nevertheless, he understands that it is his responsibility to make sure she, or any other guest of his, is introduced to people whom she does not already know.

A gentleman does not dawdle in
the receiving line.

———

A gentleman knows that "Thank you so
much for including me," "What a happy
evening," or "Don't you look lovely?"
is all the chitchat necessary in any
receiving line.

———

When going through the receiving
line, a gentleman may indeed seize
the opportunity to give the bride a
congratulatory peck on the cheek,
provided she and he are already
friends. (A gentleman does not make
it a practice to kiss women on their
cheeks, immediately upon being
introduced to them.)

———

A gentleman may also kiss the
bridesmaids.

V.

DRESSING FOR THE DAY

*What to Wear, When to Wear It,
How to Wear It*

Uniform Behavior

Every gentleman in any wedding party—from the groom down to the ring bearer—does his best to look his best for the wedding ceremony.

————

While a gentleman is honored to be a member of a good friend's wedding party, he understands that, appearance-wise, his essential function is to accessorize the bride.

————

When the suits for his attendants are being selected, the groom recommends the correct attire for the time of day and style of the ceremony.

————

Working together with the bride, the groom selects the attire in which his attendants will look their handsomest.

Early in the game, if he is not fully comfortable with the bride's suiting suggestions, the groom will be wise to ask, "Are we really sure green brocade is the right thing for Porky Tenpenny?"

———

If a gentleman has a vision of his groomsmen dressed in outfits inspired by a recent movie, a sports team, or the members of a rock band, he thinks again.

———

Unless the traditions of his faith, or the bride's faith, require that gentlemen cover their heads during the ceremony, a groom does not suggest that the members of his party be allowed to wear hats—especially not cowboy hats or baseball caps, even more especially baseball caps that have been turned backward.

———

Unless his wedding is taking place in the midst of a mudslide, a gentleman does not wear lug soles during the ceremony.

DRESSING FOR THE DAY

Unless his wedding is taking place on a basketball court, a gentleman does not wear any sort of athletic shoes during the ceremony.

———————

If a gentleman is a member of a wedding party, he does not overload his trouser pockets. It is highly unlikely he will need his key ring, his cell phone, or his Swiss army knife over the course of the wedding ceremony.

———————

If a gentleman does not own the right shoes, he borrows them.

———————

When being fitted for his formalwear, a gentleman checks to make sure all necessary accessories (including shoes, tie, cuff links and studs, and vest or cummerbund) come as part of the rental package.

———————

A gentleman picks up his suit at least 48 hours before the day of the ceremony.

Before he walks out of the rental store, a gentleman tries on his suit. If it does not fit, he does not say, "Well, I guess this will have to be okay."

———————

If his suit does not fit, a gentleman says, "Before I leave the store, let's make it right."

If any of the measurements of his suit are wrong, a gentleman requests that it be altered and ready for pickup well before the morning of the wedding day.

———————

In every case, when he has agreed to be part of a wedding party, a gentleman knows what he is expected to wear, well ahead of time. If he has questions, he asks them, self-confidently, and with no trepidation.

In a Fit

Knowing What to Wear

As soon as possible after accepting the honor of joining a friend's wedding party, a gentleman makes sure he correctly understands the dress code for the ceremony (as well as the dress codes for other events surrounding the wedding).

Ideally, the groom will set such concerns to rest, immediately assuring his attendants-to-be that the best man will be in contact shortly, providing all pertinent details. It is traditionally the best man's responsibility to coordinate all formalwear rentals and to handle their returns as expeditiously as possible in the wake of the ceremony. However, and especially if the best man is an out-of-towner, some other member of the groom's wedding party may take on these duties. In some cases, inevitably, the mother of the bride will wish to oversee these, and all other, matters.

The groom always makes sure, however, that his attendants know the correct source for information regarding the upcoming festivities.

Should a gentleman fear that he may be left in the lurch about wardrobe-related matters, he simply asks, "What will we be wearing?" (In no case does he ask, "What is this going to cost me?") The groom then replies by saying, "Gastonelli's on Fourth Street will be handling the rentals; they already have the details on file." Or he says, "Darren Plotkus has agreed to be my best man, so he'll know all those details. You'll be hearing from him in the next few days, but let me give you his phone number and his e-mail address, so the two of you can be in touch."

In short order, the best man calls or e-mails each of the potential groomsmen/ushers to let them know where and how their suits can be rented. In the best of all cases, the dress code for the wedding party will be straightforward "black tie," so there will be very few questions to answer.

In fact, if the groom and his friends already have active social lives and burgeoning business careers, some of the wedding party may already own their own formalwear (yet another reason for sticking with traditional tuxedos). But this will seldom be the case, making the selection of a dependable, respected formalwear rental firm a vital part of the planning for the wedding day.

If some members of the wedding party (perhaps even including the groom) are from out of town, it may be advisable to use a reputable rental company with locations in a number of cities. That way, each gentleman can be confident that his suit fits properly before he heads out for a busy wedding weekend.

Most likely, should there be any problem with the tailoring, the local store will be able to assist him. What's more, the local store will probably accept the return of all suits from a store in the chain. At any rate, the best man will be wise to check on company policy regarding such matters, well ahead of time.

The groom's parents, the bride's parents, or

the groom himself may elect to pay for the rental of formalwear for the groom's attendants. Unless he has heard otherwise, however, the groomsman/usher assumes that he is paying for the rental of his own suit.

In some instances—particularly when the ceremony takes place in mid-afternoon—all the gentlemen in the wedding may be asked to wear identical blazers or matching suits. If such is the case, a thoughtful bride and groom will select jackets or suits that are readily available, reasonably priced, and useful for any number of other occasions.

If the dress code for the ceremony requires the purchase of matching ties, socks, and/or pocket squares, the groom covers those expenses. He considers them simply as gifts from him to the gentlemen who have stood by his side.

Tradition holds that it is the groom's responsibility to provide ties and gloves for all his attendants. These days, however, ties and gloves are usually included along with the rest of the attendant's rented formalwear. (Gloves are worn at only the most scrupulously formal, meticulously traditional ceremonies.) If the wedding is more informal, and the bride wishes all the gentlemen to wear matching ties to go with their business suits or blazers, again, it is the groom's obligation to cover the cost.

Suited to the Occasion

If the bride and groom envision a traditional wedding ceremony, there will be little question about the attire any of the gentlemen involved in the ceremony. For a formal wedding, gray tailcoats or frock coats (with complementary accessories) are worn before noon; gray sports-coat-length jackets, known as "strollers" or "boulevards," are worn in the afternoon; and black tie is worn after six. For extremely formal weddings, when the actual ceremony does not begin until seven or seven thirty, the bride and groom may choose for his attendants to wear white tie. (Various types of formalwear are illustrated on pages 178–180.)

If the ceremony is less formal, or if it takes place in the late afternoon (between five and six o'clock, for example), the groom may suggest that his attendants simply wear dignified suits, or blazers and slacks. With the assistance of the best man, he helps all the gentlemen in his party coordinate their outfits, even if it means that one of his attendants must buy, or borrow, a suit or blazer.

If the wedding ceremony is extremely informal, or even casual, members of the groom's party will have much more leeway when it comes to deciding what to wear. Nevertheless, a foresightful groom will ask his best man to check with each member of his wedding party, lest the bride break into tears on her wedding day, at the unexpected spectacle of a groomsman in a tank top and sandals.

IS IT TUX TIME YET?

An hour-by-hour guide to appropriate attire for gentlemen in the wedding party

Dressing for Weddings . . .

The wedding begins at	The invitation was
11 A.M.	engraved or thermographed
1 P.M.	engraved or thermographed
4 P.M.	handmade by the bride
5:30 P.M.	printed
5:30 P.M.	engraved
7 P.M.	obviously engraved

Anywhere, Any Place

The Reception Will Be Held In	A Gentleman Wears
A university club, a hotel, or a private social club	Morning coats (gray tailcoats) with striped trousers, broad ties, and dove-gray waistcoats
A university club, the church's parish hall, a hotel reception room, or a private social club	"Stroller" or "Boulevard" (sports-coat-length) jackets and striped trousers, with dove-gray waistcoats and simple, broad ties
The home of the bride's parents or on a beachhead overlooking the sea	Linen jackets or whatever guise the bride and groom have decreed
A university club, a church hall, a hotel reception room, or a private club	Dark suits, or matching blazers and slacks, depending on the time of year
A private club, a private home, or a hotel reception room	Black tie
A private club, a private home, or a hotel reception room	White tie

The "Morning Coat" (aka the "Cutaway")

correct for ceremonies beginning between 10:30 A.M. and 12:30 P.M.

worn with:

white wing-collar shirt, Windsor, or ascot-style tie

white pocket square (cotton or linen)

gray vest

black or pearl-gray cuff links

gray and white–striped trousers, uncuffed

black or dark-gray socks

black, patent-leather lace-up oxfords

The "Stroller"

correct for ceremonies beginning between 3 P.M. and 5 P.M.

worn with:

white wing-collar shirt

four-in-hand, Windsor, or ascot-style tie

white pocket square (cotton or linen)

gray vest

black or pearl-gray cuff links

gray and white–striped trousers, uncuffed

black or dark-gray socks

black, patent-leather lace-up oxfords

The Tuxedo (aka "Black Tie")
correct for ceremonies beginning after 5:30 P.M.

worn with:

white wing-collar shirt or white
    soft-collar shirt with pleated
    front
black bow tie
white pocket square
black vest or cummerbund
black shirt studs and cuff links
black trousers with a satin stripe
black socks
black, patent-leather lace-up
    oxfords or formal patent-
    leather pumps

The Tailcoat (aka "White Tie")
correct for ceremonies beginning at 7 P.M. (but no earlier)

worn with:

white wing-collar shirt with piqué
    front*
white cotton piqué or linen piqué tie
white cotton or linen pocket square
white cotton or linen piqué vest
white or pearl shirt studs and cuff
    links
black trousers with a satin stripe
black socks
black, patent-leather plain-toed
    shoes

---

*Piqué is a heavily starched, white cotton or linen fabric, woven in a square-web pattern. It provides the crispest look possible, for formal occasions.

The Business Suit
correct at all hours

worn with:

white soft-collar shirt (not
    button-down) with button
    front

four-in-hand, Windsor, or bow tie

pocket square, either white or
    complementing (not precisely
    matching) the tie

simple cuff links (perhaps a gift
    from the groom)

belt or suspenders (*never* both)

black or gray socks, perhaps with
    a subtle pattern

freshly shined black leather
    shoes, with leather soles

White Nights

Although the white dinner jacket is treated with irrational disdain in some circles, it remains absolutely correct, attractive, and appropriate for weddings held in the summer and at resorts, particularly if the ceremony is held outdoors, and if it begins after six in the evening. (It is virtually interchangeable with the black dinner jacket, on such occasions.)

Let it be noted, however, that, in order for it to be correct, a white dinner jacket is never precisely white. Instead, it is a creamy off-white or a pale ivory. It is worn with the traditional black bow tie, black cummerbund, and black trousers. What's more, it must be worn with absolute self-confidence. If a gentleman has the personal nonchalance required by such a jacket, he can ease himself into an elegant evening. Otherwise, he runs the risk of looking like a member of a 1940s dance band. Or, even worse, a seventeen-year-old on his way to the prom.

If it is at all possible, a gentleman ties
his own bow tie, even if a pre-tied
bow tie is included with his
rented formalwear.

———

If a gentleman has never before
tied his own bow tie, he starts
practicing several days, maybe
even weeks, in advance.

———

Even if he is well-experienced in the
art of bow-tying, a gentleman does not
attempt to tie his bow tie in a hurry.
On a hectic day such as this,
a gentleman allows himself ample
time to tie his tie, whether it is a bow
tie or a simple four-in-hand.

How to Tie a Bow Tie

Tying a bow tie is, essentially, like tying any other bow. A gentleman knows this, and he does not become frustrated if he fumbles the first few times he attempts the procedure. Instead, he gives himself enough practice at home when he does not have a pressing dinner date.

1. Adjust the length of the tie. (A shorter tie will result in a smaller bow. If the tie is left long, the end product has a fluffier, less-tailored look.)

2. Put the tie around your neck. Leave one end hanging longer than the other.

3. Bring the long end of the tie over the short end. Then pull it up from behind, just as if you were beginning a granny knot.

4. Tug securely on both ends.

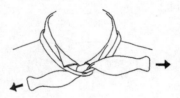

5. Fold the short end of the tie over to make a loop.

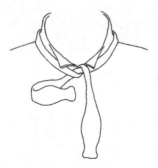

6. Bring the long end of the tie up, over, and around the middle of the entire package.

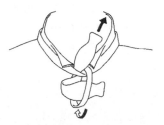

7. Fold the remaining part of the long end into a loop and stuff it through the opening behind the short end. (The loop of the long end must end up behind the flat part of the short end.)

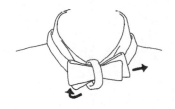

8. Tug on the tie and twist it about until it takes on a neatly finished look. (This step may take some time, but do not give up. It really will work. Just remember to tug on both loops at the same time, just as if you were tightening your shoe-laces. Otherwise, the bow will come undone.)

When wearing a bow tie with a wing-collar shirt, a gentleman wears the "wings" of the collar behind the tie.

————

When wearing a vest, as part of formalwear or otherwise, a gentleman always leaves at least one of its bottom buttons unbuttoned.

————

If a gentleman in a wedding party wears a vest with his formalwear, he leaves his jacket unbuttoned.

————

If a gentleman in a wedding party wears a cummerbund with his formalwear, he buttons the middle button of his jacket, at least for the duration of the ceremony.

When wearing a cummerbund,
a gentleman makes sure that the pleats
are turned upward, forming little
pockets, handy for the stashing of a
valet-parking stub, a theater ticket,
or even a car key.

————

A gentleman never wears suspenders
and a belt at the same time, even if he
is wearing a cummerbund to cover
all the hardware.

————

If a gentleman is wearing a vest
with his suit, he leaves all his jacket
buttons unbuttoned.

————

The groom, as well as any other
gentleman taking part in the
wedding ceremony, schedules
himself for a haircut at least two
days before the ceremony.

If a gentleman in the wedding party
is an out-of-towner, he schedules his
haircut with his own hairstylist, before
he leaves his own town, in order to
avoid subjecting his head to an
unfamiliar pair of scissors.

———————

Before heading to the wedding ceremony,
or to any other event involved in the
wedding celebration, a gentleman makes
sure his shoes are shined.

———————

Before heading to the wedding
ceremony, a gentleman takes a last-
minute inventory of his appearance,
making sure his fingernails are clean,
his fly is zipped, and his ears are free
of shaving cream.

Before heading out for the wedding ceremony, every gentleman in the wedding party makes sure to equip himself with a fresh pocket handkerchief, or even two, since he knows he may very likely be called upon to assist at least one wedding guest brought to tears by this moment of joy.

VI.

TERROR IN A TUXEDO

*10 Wedding Day Disasters,
and How to Avoid Them*

No wedding day is ultimately a disaster. At the very least, it is fodder for good stories that parents, groomsmen, ushers, guests, children, and grandchildren can pass along for generations to come.

Nevertheless, the well-equipped groom is ready to face any number of awkward eventualities. Love may conquer all—eventually. But when there are speed bumps on the way to the altar, a bit of level-headed advice also comes in handy.

WHAT TO DO . . .

If the groom finds himself (and his bride) caught between feuding families:

The groom does his best to serve as peacemaker, at least if the trouble seems to be brewing on his side of the aisle. He meets privately with the disgruntled parties—who may be his parents, his grandparents, a surly sibling, or even an overly outspoken cousin— saying, "Maureen and I love each other, and we plan to spend the rest of our lives together. We both hope you will be a part of our wedding day and all the years that lie ahead."

Should the unhappiness seem to be originating among the bride's relations, he encourages her to attempt the same strategy, standing alongside her and holding her hand firmly, should she ask him to do so.

In no instance does he stir the waters by carrying tales back and forth between the families. Neither does he unnecessarily distress the bride with teapot-sized tempests that are likely to blow over once the wedding plans are under way.

If the rift appears to be irreparable, the groom and bride face that unpleasant reality together. Especially if either set of parents is proving problematic, they meet with them quietly in a private place—*not* a crowded restaurant or a cocktail lounge—reaffirming their intent to be married and their love for each other.

If the conversation does not go well, they do not toss down the gauntlet and stalk out of the room, leaving "Well, we're getting married anyhow, whether you like it or not" as their parting shot. Instead, they say, "We love you, and we hope you'll feel differently someday." Then they proceed to plan their wedding, and the rest of their lives together.

Under no circumstances does the groom, or the bride, attempt to tackle this sort of testy situation via e-mail, much less any sort of online social network. Ungainly family affairs are most often best handled face-to-face. They have no place in the public forum.

If the groom finds that his own mother is feeling neglected as the wedding grows near:

If the bride's family is taking the lead in all plans for the wedding, even the most well-meaning mother of the groom may find herself feeling more than a little like an outsider. Such feelings may even be exacerbated if she has no daughters of her own and, thus, will never have the opportunity to fill the mother-of-the-bride's slippers.

As the wedding day approaches, the groom does his best to remain attentive to all the women in his life. (It will be good practice for his life as a married man.) He does not simply assume that his mother will tell him how she feels, if she is feeling less than happy. He finds time to spend with his mother—just the two of them.

He does his best to help his mother and the bride get to know each other, which does not mean he expects them to become best friends. Instead, he hopes they will learn to love each other, not least because they both share a love for him. He also enlists the bride's assistance in making sure his mother and her own are on pleasant terms, encouraging her to keep her future mother-in-law in the loop as the planning proceeds. For instance, it will be only thoughtful for her to share decisions regarding color choices, flowers, and the reception menu.

Nevertheless, it may become his responsibility to run interference, should his mother not be a good team player. If she is finding it difficult to winnow her guest list to the number she has been offered, for example, he offers to help with the editing. "Why don't we work on this together." he may suggest. That, after all, is what a loving son would do.

If the bride hears tales of ungentlemanly behavior at the bachelor bash:

It is the groom's responsibility, of course, to make sure

that such tales are untrue, at least insofar as they involve his own behavior.

Although he is the guest of honor at the bachelor party, and although he does not wish to be thought a prig, he also remembers that, if there are any wild oats left to sow, they probably should not be his own. When the partying gets particularly raucous, in fact, he and the best man may be wise to leave the room. That way, if pictures involving scantily clad persons happen to show up on the Internet, the groom will be able to say, with a clear conscience, "Well, yes, I saw those pictures too. I bet Bobo Torkqvist is sorry Harry Hallstein brought his camera."

Better yet, he will not be left coming up with outmoded "boys will be boys" excuses for the behavior of others. Best of all, he will have no apologies to make.

If the groom discovers that he (or the best man) has lost the ring:

If the bride's ring has somehow gone missing, the groom will be lucky to know about it before he is in the midst of the ceremony. Given enough lead time, he may borrow a ring from a helpful and handy friend or relation, making sure the bride is aware of the temporary substitution.

Should the ring turn up missing at the very moment when it is to be slipped effortlessly on the bride's finger, there is little that can be done except for the groom or best man to inform the officiant about the situation— either by way of the subtlest sort of whispering or the least demonstrative raising of eyebrows. The officiant will know what to do, probably proceeding with a pantomime exchange of rings.

The bride will be less than content with the pretense. But, should the ring not turn up before the end of the reception, the groom assures her that a visit to a jeweler has just been added to the itinerary for their honeymoon.

If someone actually should stand up at the ceremony and declare that there is indeed "a reason this man and this woman should not be joined in marriage":

It is difficult to imagine any just cause for such a calamity, unless it should turn out that either the bride or the groom is, in fact, already married. If such should be the reality, there is no option except for the ceremony to cease, the guests to depart, and the caterer to pack up the wedding cake.

A protest that "Larry owes me 150 bucks!" or "Tiffany's still got my class ring!" while an inconvenience, is no cause to cancel the ceremony. It is, instead, a cause for a couple of able-bodied groomsmen to calmly escort the distracted party from the building.

If a member of the groom's wedding party shows up, obviously still suffering the aftereffects of the previous night's partying:

It's doubtful that anyone considers a staggering, green-gilled groomsman to be an even remotely amusing spectacle, especially if his behavior threatens to sabotage a celebration that has been months, maybe even years, in the planning. For that reason, every gentleman involved in the wedding party carefully monitors his own behavior, and his alcohol intake, at the rehearsal dinner, and—perhaps even more important—in the hours following it. (The ill-advised tradition of holding the groom's bachelor party in the wake of the rehearsal dinner has, with good reason, fallen by the wayside.)

Should a still-besotted groomsman or usher show up, expecting to escort ladies down the aisle, it is the best man—who is there to serve as the alpha dog of the wedding pack, who must spring to action—assessing the situation and doing his best to determine whether the fellow is indeed capable of fulfilling his responsibilities. This is no moment for berating him for his misbehavior. The job is to save the moment.

If it appears that the fellow clearly is not up to the task, or if he has not even shown up, and the onset of the ceremony is scarcely a half hour away, the best man first informs the wedding coordinator, who then carries the news to the mother of the bride. If worse comes to worst, the processional may have to be rearranged.

Not only will the derelict groomsman find himself left out of the lineup; he may rightfully expect to be left out of the newlyweds' lives until further notice.

All the gentlemen involved in the wedding party will find themselves well-advised to remember that "I do" and "Sure, I'll have another" may well make for an unfortunate mix.

If children, perhaps disapproving, from previous marriages are involved in the ceremony:

Many is the modern wedding that comes pre-equipped with children, from either one or both of the spouses' previous relationships. Sometimes those children are wee sprites, adored by one and all; sometimes they are teens who've never worn a tie or been asked to turn off their cell phones; sometimes they are full-grown, and full of their own opinions.

In an ideal world, a grandparent, an all-accepting aunt, or even a nanny will be available to keep a grip on any tiny tots—and to see that they are trundled home, perhaps after one cup of (unspiked) punch at the party. (Maybe they can be given their own precisely portioned take-home mini wedding cakes.)

Tweens and teens may actually acquiesce to behave themselves, perhaps even joining the wedding party as junior bridesmaids or junior groomsmen. If they are invited to bring a couple (but only a couple) of friends along to the reception, their acquiescence may be easier to obtain.

If the spouses-to-be are both on good terms with the children, they may rejoice in asking the entire tribe to join in the celebration. However, if ill will is wafting on the wind (stirred up either by the children themselves or by a party-pooping ex), the invitation may be an awkward one. Nevertheless, the offer must be made.

If the groom is on less-than-pleasant terms with his ex, and if a young child is involved, he may broach the subject (face-to-face or by telephone, *not* by any means of electronic communication) by suggesting, "I'm hoping Jessica will be able to come along to the wedding with Mom [or Aunt Tabitha or Cousin Sandy]." If communication with the former spouse is an impossibility, he may call upon his mother, or Aunt Tabitha or Cousin Sandy, to serve as an intermediary.

Asking children from one side of the relationship to be involved in the ceremony, while neglecting or, even worse, excluding children from the other side, is a prescription for disaster. The new family—now joined together from what were previously two separate families—will have to live with the decisions of this wedding day forever, no matter what the future holds. (A gentleman knows that no one day is truly happy if it spells disaster for generations to come.)

If the bride goes ballistic as the wedding day grows near:

There are endless stories of brides gone bad—tales of seemingly sane, absolutely reasonable women who crack up, at least temporarily, in anticipation of the most joyous day of their lives.

The groom-to-be may find himself a witness to such a moment, but he need not see himself as its victim. The tensions that lead to tears may very likely have little, if anything, to do with him. They may, in fact, have to do with mother-daughter disagreements. They may have to do with the color of the tulips. They may have to do with the zipper on the dress.

In such situations, which are almost invariably related to stress, the groom has little option except to ask, "What can I do to help?" If the bride's seemingly irrational response is, "How could you possibly help anything?" his calming comeback is, "I'm here for you, honey. Why don't we talk this through?"

He may wish to consult the bride's mother, or maybe her father, to determine if the situation is actually dire. And he may wish to vent by sharing his travails with the best man, or some other trustworthy friend. He does not share his "bridezilla" tales on the Internet.

But his best option may be simply to say, "Let's take a break tonight, just the two of us, and go out for dinner. Let's find someplace where we can get a quiet little table with candles and a nice bottle of wine."

If the bride turns indecisive, at the very last minute:

Instances of cold feet on the way to the altar are not unheard-of. Should he be subjected to such a moment, the groom will find little profit in attempting to reason with the bride. Questions such as "What's wrong?" "Don't you love me?" and "Don't you know there are 250 people waiting out there?" will inevitably prove fruitless, just minutes before the ceremony is set to begin.

The groom's best option is to ask that the maid of honor, the bride's mother or father, or even the minister intervene. He gives the bride a gentle kiss; tells her, "I love you"; and steals quietly from the room, fully confident that the next time he sees her, she will be radiant and smiling, looking into his eyes as she walks down the aisle.

Unless the bride chooses, someday in the distant future, to recall this anxious ungainliness, he never mentions the moment again.

If the groom forgets his vows in the midst of the ceremony:

There is a reason the officiant usually says, "Repeat after me . . ."

If the groom has elected to write his own vows, he brings a hard copy along with him to the ceremony. He does not trust his faltering memory on a day he will remember for the rest of his life.

INDEX

bow tie, 182
    how to tie, 183–186
    with wing-collar shirt, 187
bride-to-be
    groom's gift to, 50
    indecision, 200–201
    name after wedding, 26
    relationship with groom's mother, 194
    stress, 199–200
bride's bouquet, tossing, 59
bride's dress, 31, 44, 113
    responsibility for expense, 104, 108
brothers, of groom, 32
budget, 11–12. *See also* expenses
    for engagement ring, 19
    for wedding, 104–105
business suit, 180

C

cameras, 144
carat, 20
cash, as gift, 156–157
casual wedding ceremony, clothes for, 175
cell phones, 148
children, from previous marriage, 198–199
civil marriage ceremony, 37
clarity of diamond, 20
clothes, 168–190
    for bachelor party, 89
    for casual wedding ceremony, 175
    guidelines, 168–190
    for honeymoon, 60–61
    hour-by-hour guide, 176–177
    for wedding guest, 150, 151
clothes for bridal party, 168–169. *See also* formalwear
    asking for guidance, 78, 171, 172
cold feet, 200–201
color of diamond, 20
comments about marriage, 163–164
communicating reply to wedding invitation, 137–138
"congratulations," vs. "best wishes," 149

H

P

parents of fiancée
 addressing, 5
 groom and, 2–3
parents, problems from, 193
parties, 156–157. *See also* bachelor party
photographs, 44–45, 144, 165
 of bachelor party, 92
picture frames, as gifts, 155
pleats on cummerbund, 188
pranks, 87
prenuptial counseling, 36
private wedding ceremony, 24

Q

quiet wedding ceremony, 24

R

"reason for not joining in marriage," expression of, 196
receiving line, 116–117, 165
reception. *See* wedding reception
registering for wedding gifts, 47, 153
rehearsal dinner
 father of groom as host, 120
 groom and, 53
religious community, and selecting minister, 36–37
religious service, guest participation in wedding as, 142
remote weddings, 54–55
rental of formalwear, 170–171
ringbearer, 94–95
round diamond cut, 21

S

seating at wedding, 13
shoes, 169–170, 189
shotgun wedding, 23
showers for bride, 53, 156–157
"significant other," request to include as wedding guest, 143–144
sitting "within the ribbons," 146
sports-coat-length jackets, 175

vest, 187, 188
vows
    forgetting during ceremony, 201
    practicing, 38
    writing, 38
    written copy of, 39–40

W

wedding, ix
    budget for, 104–105
    responsibility for expenses, 10–12
wedding anniversaries, classic gifts for, 62–63
wedding ceremony
    departing at conclusion, 147
    forgetting vows during, 201
    instructions for groom, 3
    objections during, 196
    photographs during, 45
    recommended arrival time, 142
    untraditional, 158–159
wedding day
    selecting, 30–31
    timeline, 98–99
wedding dress, 31, 44, 113
    responsibility for expense, 104, 108
wedding party, selecting members of, 32–34
wedding planner, 4
wedding plans, groom's concerns, 4
wedding reception, 13, 164
    groom and, 53
    phone calls during, 148
wedding rings, 9, 35
    best man's responsibility for, 77
    loss of, 195–196
white dinner jacket, 181
white tie, 175, 177, 179
wing-collar shirt, bow tie with, 187
worship service, photographs during, 45

Y

yarmulke, 142